On The Shoulders
OF LEADERS

-A Leadership Pocket Guide

In the end; leadership is all about people

DR. JAMES FANTAUZZO, PH.D.

Xulon
ELITE

To contact the author:

Dr. James Fantauzzo
Cts7349@msn.com
(772) 359 - 0041

www.xulonpress.com

About the Author

D r. James Fantauzzo, President of Creative Training Solutions, is one of America's most dynamic Management Consultants and Human Resources experts.

For the past twenty-five years he has provided professional services for the health care, manufacturing, and hospitality industries as well as academia. As a consultant, trainer, speaker, and author, Dr. Fantauzzo has helped companies overcome organizational performance concerns in the areas related to training and development, team building, employee relations, customer service, and leadership. Jim has received national recognition as a speaker and presenter of seminars and workshops as referenced by his testimonials. He has earned the reputation of helping companies solve their employee organizational concerns. He is also a member of the Christian Coaches Network and the National Speakers Association.

In addition to servicing various industries, he has taught at the undergraduate and post-graduate levels for several universities in the School of Business for many years. Dr. Fantauzzo continues to devote his time and energy in assisting organizations and their people to improve their leadership responsibilities.

Acknowledgements

This book is dedicated to the many individuals, peers, teachers, family and friends who have influenced my writing development. I am indebted to the many fine people I have had the privilege of working with and serving. So much of my knowledge came from research, clients, teaching and colleagues.

I also want to thank Lara Wright for her technical computer competence, support, and overall knowledge.

In this regard, the journey began from a manuscript to the finished product to give the business world something of high utility, realism, and value.

With special thanks to my wife Linda and children, Tim, Todd, and Stacey, who helped me to continue dreaming and with their hope for the dreams my children will have. Your love, joy and happiness has brought a sense of accomplishment to my life.

I want to give special thanks to all the men and women who have opened their hearts and shared their leadership stories with me. Your commitment to leadership and people will make the business world a better place.

Testimonials

I just wanted to express my sincere appreciation for the dedication that you have shown to the educational program here at Heritage Christian Home. Your sincerity and wisdom is felt immediately by the participants. You speak from the heart with passion and commitment and that is irreplaceable.

> Marisa E. Geitner, Organizational Development
> Heritage Christian Home

We thank you very much for speaking at the FLAILM Annual Educational Conference. I have received very positive responses and the recommendation that you be asked back.

> James R. Stine, Conference Co-Chairman
> Tingue, Brown & Co.

I would like to thank you for the excellent training, *The Art of Exceeding Customer Expectations in Healthcare*. The participants found the training to be interesting, informative and very useful for their performance as marketing and customer service executives.

> Nanette M. Dumont, Executive Assistant
> Triple-S, Inc. Blue Cross and Blue Shield of Puerto Rico

I find Jim to be extremely compassionate, responsive and always professional in his facilitation. Jim's materials are concise and carefully prepared. He holds his audience's attention and the evaluations we receive are always favorable and extremely complimentary of Jim's style of delivery.

> Saralie R. Foote, Manager, Training
> Industrial Management Council

Thank you! Your presentation on *Improving Teamwork: Voyage to Excellence* at our chapter meeting of IAAP was wonderful. We have heard nothing but positive feedback since our meeting.

> Erika J. Kemblowski, CPS, Vice-President
> Flower City Chapter IAAP

Dr. James Fantauzzo serves as a Human Resources Consultant to Optical Gaging Productions, Inc. Jim has modernized and streamlined our staffing selection process, personnel training, and development, appraisal, and feedback system by providing specific recommendations on how to improve each area of the work environment.

His management style and leadership efforts have generated far-reaching improvements in our corporate culture.

Our managers have a higher level of awareness and effectiveness regarding the human resources that they control. Jim's recommendations resulted in significant cost savings to the corporation.

We now have a program that has reduced our cost of hiring. We have a system that co-ordinates manpower needs and the staff available, taking greater advantage of our ability to promote from within the corporations.

Edward T. Polidor, President
Optical Gaging Products, Inc.

Dear Dr. Fantauzzo,

I wanted to take this opportunity to thank you for the excellent presentation you did for our October 15, 1997, Western New York Educational Conference. The entire group of attendees very well received the two seminars.

It was also very much appreciated at how you tailored these two areas specifically to not only to the health care industry, but also specifically to individuals in our profession. This gave greater meaning, and I believe greater participation, to our Conference. I look forward to the possibility of having you again in the future.

Terry Cole, Conference Chairman
The McGuire Group

Dear Dr. Fantauzzo,

I am writing to thank you again for your generous gesture in providing our staff with the wonderful leadership training on May 2, 2003. We are all trying to put the valuable information to work. I personally have begun looking at our evaluation and feedback policies and have been considering some of your suggestions. I have also decided to use "art mart" at our next directors' meeting on May 30. It was my favorite part of the training. Thank you again.

Sheila Young, S.A.I.L. Coordinator
Kids' Harbor Preschool & Child Care

Dear Dr. Fantauzzo,

First I would like to compliment you on a fine presentation at the Customer Satisfaction Conference in Washington, D.C., last month. Not only was your presentation content meaningful but your treatment of adult learning theory was impeccable.

Dr. Fantauzzo, It was refreshing to see someone so confident in their own professional station to allow others, such as myself, to offer our experience without cutting us off or diminishing the effect of your wonderful presentation. Your ability to think on your feet and maintain a significant presence in the room was simply remarkable.

Michael P. Grinnals, Director of Education & Training,
Thompson Health

Dear Dr. Fantauzzo,

On behalf of the staff at Melles Griot Optical Systems, I would like to take this opportunity to thank you for the excellent training you have provided. The participants found the weekly training sessions to be well planned, informative, and an asset to their professional careers. The skills learned during the training sessions could be instantly put to use with the day-to-day issues faced among the participants. It was apparent that a great deal of preparation went into this customized training program. Upon completion of this five-week program, the participants gained the knowledge and confidence needed to improve their skills.

Deborah Gsellmeier, Human Resources Manager

Melles Griot Optical Systems

Dear Dr. Fantauzzo:

On behalf of all the members of the Employees Communication Council, we would like to express our gratitude for all you have done for our hospital.

Although you were here for such a short time, your charisma and dynamic personality has resulted in much-needed advances toward better communication between management and employees, thus moving our institution in a positive direction.

The officers would particularly like to thank you for the extra time you gave to us. Your suggestions and guidance were appreciated.

Tillie Fulton, RN, Chairperson

Joe Lowe, Vice Chairperson

Pat Quattrone, Secretary Olean General Hospital

Dear Dr. Bottenberg,

As a recent graduate of Warren National University's doctoral program in Health Administration, I'd like to take a moment to share my gratitude and appreciation for Dr. Fanauzzo who was my dissertation advisor. Dr. Fantauzzo's knowledge, patient guidance, and leadership are outstanding. Distance learning can have its challenges for some students, but dedicated teachers like Dr. Fantauzzo make all the difference.

If it were not for Dr. Fantauzzo I might not have finished my degree. For the past seven years I have had chronic Hodgkin's Lymphoma, which requires that I periodically take chemotherapy to shrink tumors when they become too big. During the last two months of my dissertation a tumor was found behind my heart and I had to begin weekly chemotherapy. I wasn't sure if I had the physical or mental strength to continue my degree and was on the verge of giving up. Dr. Fantauzzo would not let me give up. He was the rainbow in a state of chaos. He believed in me and his belief gave me the strength to believe in myself and continue onward. Dr. Fantauzzo has become a trusted friend and mentor. I feel blessed to have had such an incredible teacher.

Dr. Michelle Miller, PhD Graduate
Warren National University

Dr. Fantauzzo has a very impressive background and experience in the areas of human resources, management, business, leadership development, motivational speaking, and he uses all of this marvelous background in the classroom.

During two different terms in the years 2000 and 2007, Dr. Fantauzzo taught

Administration 646, Human Resource Administration on the undergraduate level, at Barry University's School of Adult and Continuing Education (ACE), on the Treasure Coast. On their course evaluation forms, the students said that they found their instructor to be very knowledgeable of the subject area, and an excellent source of information. There was general agreement that the course was well taught, and that Dr. Fantauzzo really cared about his students. Several mentioned that they would definitely take another course from this instructor should the opportunity present itself.

I personally observed Dr. Fantauzzo in the ACE classroom and found him to be well prepared, and there was good inter-action and rapport between instructor and students. It was obvious that Jim loved being in the classroom, helping students to acquire new knowledge that would be helpful to them on both professional and personal levels. We hope to schedule Dr. Fantauzzo for another class in the near future.

Sister Grace Flowers, OP
Associate Director and Student Advisor
Barry University, School of Adult and
Continuing Education

"I would like to offer this letter of recommendation for Dr. James Fantauzzo. Dr. Fantauzzo has been a faculty member in the School of Business at Warner Southern for the past several years. He has taught a number of different courses at the undergraduate and graduate levels on management and leadership. Dr. Fantauzzo's students have always rated him as one of their best professors. During his time here, he has been a contributing member of the faculty and the school.

In addition to his abilities as a faculty member, I have found him to be of the highest character."

William M. Rigel,
PhD Executive Vice President and Chief Academic
Officer Warner Southern University

Foreword

In putting together *On The Shoulders of Leaders* it was my goal and purpose to offer practical daily leadership wisdom, advice, and inspiration to meet the many challenges in our daily work lives.

If you are a supervisor, manager, director, vice-president, president, trainer, consultant, coach or student, or a military leader, then by design this book was written for you.

The ideas, research, and the preparation of this book required patience, careful thought and analysis, and continuous editing. Perhaps one of the most important factors was the belief that this book would provide realistic and useful information to help all managers—current and future—to understand the importance of proactive and effective leadership.

The contents of the book have been prepared for managers of all disciplines. The approaches are related to business strategies and proven ideas that are the result of my experience as a management consultant, speaker, trainer, and as a Corporate Human Resource professional in the real world of business.

In the final analysis, the purpose of leadership is to demonstrate commitment to the success of the people they lead, to earn their trust, and to treat them with respect. Your success starts with theirs.

I am pleased you are reading *On The Shoulders of Leaders*. I expect many of you will use this book throughout the years. You will want to reference certain sections again and again to review the information that will relate to the various leadership issues you are dealing with at the time. It is my hope you will consider staying in touch with me to let me know what has worked for you as a leader.

I am available to assist organizations in health care, manufacturing, hospitality, and academia. I devote my time and energy to helping organizations and people to improve their leadership responsibilities.

The best way to reach me is by e-mail: cts7349@msn.com. I also have information through my website: www.creativetrainingsolutions.net.

Introduction

Prescription for Leadership: The Purpose of Driven Leadership

O n the *Shoulders of Leaders* is a book for leaders at every level of awareness and who aspire to lead.

The business need for pro-active leadership in all segments of business is critically important for today and tomorrow. The primary purpose of the hands-on easy reference Pocket Guide is designed to assist managers at all levels to fully utilize those skills necessary to run the business each and every day. Additionally, the lack of skills and experience may have a negative impact on the employees who are under the supervision of a particular manager. In putting together the Leadership Pocket Guide, it was my intention to have it become an easy-to-use, realistic reference that would assist each manager in his or her various administrative and operational responsibilities.

In the "real world of business" today, managers are extremely busy professionals.

The *Leadership Pocket Guide* will assist them in accomplishing the day-to-day responsibilities effectively with a time-sensitive approach. In today's business world there is a significant need for pro-active leadership at all levels within the organization. Today, many management people do not have the necessary training in order to be effective leaders. Talent is helpful in a leadership role; however, commitment, believability, tenacity, and continuous training are also necessary in order to be effective. The purpose of leadership is to take responsibility for the organization and to make the Vision and Mission Statements a reality.

The basic *"How To's" Leadership Pocket Guide* has been prepared for those individuals who have a desire to improve their leadership skills and who have a desire to make a difference through their daily contribution within the scope of their role as managers. The *Leadership Pocket Guide* will define and embrace a clear understanding of how to practice sound leadership concepts. Acquiring new knowledge is important. However, how the concepts are used is even more important.

This Pocket Guide in its most simplistic form will reference numerous key components that will help management individuals to perform much more efficiently in meeting and exceeding the goals of the organization.

What this *Leadership Pocket Guide* will do for you:

The simple steps that we have set down here are not untested approaches. They are proven approaches to employee and operational topics and issues that are applicable, and steps that will work effectively.

The fact that you are reading this Guide clearly indicates that you may be looking for useful tools that will improve your individual performance and overall contribution to your organization.

In every section of the Pocket Guide you will find information that is useful and realistic. In this regard, the hands-on reference will cover the basic administrative ways in which to achieve success when administering various policies and procedures or trying to resolve operational or employee problems. So, let's begin the journey that will lead you to improved performance, significant accomplishment, and more success for you and your team.

Table of Contents

Chapter 1

Organizational Goals

STRATEGIC UNDERPINNINGS

Today in business, many of the larger organizations have prepared written Vision and Mission Statements as an important strategic way in which to run the business.

The Vision and Mission Statement are linked to the culture, the strategic planning process, the customer base, and how the organization is planning to run the business near-term and long-term.

The AOP, better known as the Annual Operating Plan is defined as a strategic plan for a twelve-month period. The longer-term strategic plan is defined as a three- year period for future planning purposes. The one-year strategic plan is a process in which all of the senior managers prepare their business plans for review and submission into the strategic plan. The size and structure of the organization will determine which members of senior management will have a submission into both the annual operating plan and the long-term strategic plan. Depending on how the organization is structured, this will determine which of the senior management members submits his or her individual plans. Typically, these could include goals for Marketing, Finance, Manufacturing, Research and Development, International Business, Human Resources, and Engineering.

Once these plans are submitted, reviewed, and finalized they will then become the final business plan for that specific year. During that year, the senior management member may be required to give quarterly reports. The purpose for doing this is to update the entire senior management team with regard to the progress that has been made or the status of each department. Based upon this report, adjustments may be made to insure that the goals of each department will be met.

It is important to note that all of the strategic plans are submitted to the president, general manager, or the corporate office for review and approval. Once again, the review and approval process will be dependent upon the culture and policies of each organization. Today's rapidly evolving world has forced many businesses to redefine themselves in an effort to build services and financial operations. They must also be masters of detail with regard to goals and strategies for future success.

Chapter 2

Trust-Building Relationships: The Voice of Leadership

CULTIVATING PEOPLE RESOURCES

Building Organizational Relationships should be an important and purposeful goal in all business cultures. If senior management makes an effort to stress the importance of this behavior throughout the organization, and makes this a part of the Vision and Mission Statements, this renewed behavior would result in higher quality and credible communication. This behavior among managers would reflect senior management's beliefs, values, and actions. Managing the environment in this manner, a stronger leadership will emerge and become more visible. When an organization harnesses the power of belief, the following changes will become visible and measurable:

- Stronger teams will be established.
- The organization's vision and mission goals will be successfully met.

- Morale will be increased.
- Greater credibility will be achieved.
- Managers and employees will exhibit more cooperation among departments.
- Customer service will be improved upon.
- Financial goals will be met or exceeded.
- Employee turnover may be reduced.
- A win-win environment will become more evident.
- Employees' positive beliefs, attitudes, and behaviors will be established as norms.

In order for any environment to function smoothly, there needs to be a high level of trust between leaders and teams of employees within each department.

Leadership through Partnership:

So much of our identity comes from our relationships. How we as leaders relate to others and how they relate to us teaches us important things about ourselves. In order for people to work effectively together, we must admit to ourselves that we need each other. Relationships will take on a much deeper meaning when people in business accept this behavioral fact.

Leadership through partnership by definition involves building teams throughout the organization in each department. This may require a paradigm shift throughout the organization. This can only be accomplished by each manager displaying pro-active leadership, commitment, and thorough, purposeful and quality communication. This paradigm shift may also require continuous auditing and accountability to insure it is making progress.

The purpose for cultivating the seeds of leadership includes:
- High Morale
- Meaningful and attainable goals
- Effective Communication
- Continuous employee training based upon a Needs Assessment Instrument
- Excellent Team Dynamics (Inter and Intra)
- State-of-the-business scheduled meetings facilitated by senior management
- Rewarding Employees
- Effective Safety Program
- Excellent Product or Service
- Profitability Objectives
- Continuous Research and Development
- Internal Employee Promotion System
- Stress Reduction Training Programs
- Employee Performance Review System
- Employee Assistance Resource Program

Talent is very helpful in leadership, but courage is also necessary.

All leaders should display patience when leading to include a situational leadership approach.[1]

---

[1] All leadership quotes by Dr. Fantauzzo

Chapter 3

Organizational Employment Recruitment

When organizations find the need to implement a recruitment plan, they normally would utilize the services of a human resources department. Quite often a human resources department would be structured in such a way that it has in place an employment manager function.

The employment manager would have the responsibility of utilizing the various methods of recruitment that would be cost effective and time sensitive. The methods of recruitment would be very dependent upon the number of openings that the organization currently has within each department. Additionally, the various openings may be categorized between hourly positions and professional positions.

The responsibility to staff all of the openings as quickly as possible would be dependent upon the Employment Manager utilizing those various methods of recruitment in an effort to attract qualified candidates. The methods of recruitment that could be approached are the following: Field Recruiting, College Recruiting, Employee Referral, Job Fair, Advertising, Open House, Employment Agency, On- Line Recruiting, and Chamber of Commerce Bulletin Boards. These various options in which to begin recruiting have withstood the test of time to be useful and effective.

Most organizations have in place an annual recruiting budget. The various financial considerations that become part of the budget preparation for each year, whether it be a fiscal or annualized calendar year is typically based upon the experience of the previous year in employee turnover. Two key points that need to be referenced are the following: a) It is extremely important that the individual(s) involved in the recruiting process be trained and gain experience conducting interviews; b) Proper placement of new hires is critically important. Having the right people in the right positions at the right time to achieve organizational objectives is very important.

If appropriate, it may be time sensitive and cost effective to conduct a telephone screen interview prior to inviting candidates in. By completing this initial assessment process, it may be determined that the candidate may not have the qualifications needed to fulfill the open position. This may save time and money for the organization, especially if there is a recruitment budget dedicated to recruiting.

Chapter 4

The Employment Interview

I t is critically important to hire the right people at the right time in which to run the business and meet organizational objectives. When a position within the organization becomes vacant, the recruiting process will begin to find a number of qualified candidates with whom to begin the interview process. If a human resources department exists within the organization, the recruiting people would take the lead in the process to pre-screen candidates before the hiring department's interview of the candidates.

Once the candidates are pre-selected and scheduled for an interview, they will begin by coming into the human resources department or the hiring department and complete the employment application form. This provides the necessary information for the interviewers to assess whether the candidate has the necessary background to fill the open position.

Ideally, in order for the interviewer to be completely prepared for the scheduled interviews, the employment application and a resume should be reviewed. This kind of preparation is required in order to conduct a professional and legal interview. By completing this important step, the interviewer will be ready to ask focused and relevant, legal questions.

Once it is determined to invite the candidate in for the interview and the candidate arrives at the scheduled date and time, the candidate should be treated as a guest during the entire interview process. This is important to insure the individual leaves the interview with a positive impression of the interviewer and the organization. There have many instances in which a candidate is treated poorly and therefore unprofessionally because the interviewer wasn't prepared or trained on how to conduct a professional interview. When this unfortunate situation takes place, the candidate may leave with a very negative impression of the interviewer and the organization.

Interviewer training should also include significant familiarization with what questions may be asked legally of each candidate and what questions should not be asked. Once again, proper placement can only be achieved if the interviewer is properly trained for this important element of the hiring process. (Please reference pages 150, 151 and 152 for visuals regarding proper interviews.)

Chapter 5

Internal Promotions

Today in various business segments a high percentage of organizations have an internal promotion policy and system that enables existing employees to get promoted into positions of greater responsibility. The administration of the Internal Promotion Policy is typically administered by a member of the Human Resources Department and the hiring manager. The process would usually begin by interviewing those employees who have requested to be considered for the open position. The initial screening would be done by a member of the Human Resources Department. Once this is completed, those employees who have the requisite skills would be scheduled to be interviewed by the hiring manager.

This policy clearly has many positive aspects related to it for the employees. It is good for morale, it provides internal growth with regard to the scope of responsibilities and pay, and it is cost effective for the company. You can use the chart below to outline your own thoughts and goals.

Team Leadership & Human Resources
Internal Promotion Goals & Objectives

_____

_____

_____

_____

_____

_____

_____

_____

_____

_____

_____

_____

_____

_____

_____

_____

_____

_____

_____

_____

_____

_____

Chapter 6

Management, Manpower, Succession Planning

The Administrative Process

The Succession Planning Process is a strategic system that embraces and approaches the manpower planning needs of an organization for the near-term and long-term. This administrative process would require the involvement of the chief executive officer (CEO), or a general manager—essentially someone who is responsible for a division, company, a hospital, or a corporation to plan for anticipated vacancies in the future.

It is a systematic staffing process that requires a great deal of analysis and planning in an effort to select the right candidate/employee to fill this vacancy. The key employees involved in the administrative process would be the senior Human Resources officer who could be a corporate director, divisional director, company manager, or director. This, of course, would depend upon how the organization is structured with regard to the reporting relationships within the organization.

This process would take place typically on an annual basis in an effort to plan for anticipated vacancies for the near-term and long-term. The near-term could be defined as Annual Operating Procedure, or a three- to five-year period. In many cases, depending upon the various operating strategies the organization has in place, this process could be integrated into the organization's business plans. This is clearly an internal recruiting and placement program structured to fill vacancies with an effective, professional, and useful internal placement procedure.

The various key steps involved in the process would be to clearly analyze the existing senior management staff who report to the president, general manager, hospital administrator, and so on in an effort to determine the following:

- Who would be retiring in the near future?
- If this person is promoted to another division within the corporation or company, who would be ready to take his or her place?
- What if this person decides to resign for better career opportunities?
- Who is ready to be promoted to take his or her place?

If a senior management position remains open for any period of time, some portion of the business will not get accomplished. This, of course, could be very problematic and far reaching and have a negative impact on business.

Once it is agreed to implement the Succession Planning Strategy for internally promoted employees and all the various administrative steps, the following steps should be included in the program:

Assessment forms should be designed for the purpose documenting profile information on various managers who could be considered for promotion. These forms should include date of hire, current salary, education, performance review information, and if they are ready to be promoted within their current discipline. If they aren't ready, determine what is needed to get them ready for a greater scope of responsibility.

This kind of analysis requires a very careful and thorough review by a trained and objective assessor. This individual would usually be the senior Human Resources officer from the corporate office, the division, or the company.

Once the assessments are completed in writing, this information normally becomes confidential and is not discussed with the employees who are candidates to be promoted at some point in the future.

Once this process begins, the organization should continue to be committed based upon the benefits of such a program. It is an important recruitment and senior management staffing strategy that could have many important benefits.

If successors cannot be identified within the organization, then outside recruiting would have to begin.

I think it is important to reference an important component with regard to internal candidates. Once internal candidates are selected and assessment determines that perhaps they aren't ready for promotion, the process would require supporting what is needed to insure that they have the needed skills to get ready. This may require going back to school, attending seminars, or both. This is part of the organization's commitment to preparing high potential successors. There are times when the employee is informed that he or she is a "high potential" candidate and there could be situations when the employee shouldn't be told. These are decisions that are made by the senior Human Resources officer and the person in charge of running the business, the President, General Manager, Corporate President, the designated person.

Unlocking the talent of high potential employees in the organization starts with a commitment to do so—the organization's commitment and the employee's commitment. For one to access one's true hidden talents one must be given the opportunity and training needed in order to find one's true authenticity. This can only be accomplished when the organization opens the door through commitment and leadership. It is better to promote people when they are ready and to run the business through this kind of a Succession Planning Strategy, which will give it life and purpose that will make a difference. It will have a positive affect on morale, motivation, productivity, team cohesiveness, turnover, and is cost-effective recruiting.

Management, Manpower, Succession Planning
Summary/Overview

This administrative process is linked to near-term and long-term planning of the manpower needed in order to run the business efficiently with qualified employees. It is a process that involves careful and professional assessment of those professional employees who have been identified as high potentials. The high potential employees are individuals who have exhibited outstanding performance in their current positions and are now ready to be promoted into positions of greater responsibilities.

This kind of planning is needed for near and long term planning in order to fill those positions that may be vacated as a result of various employees retiring, resigning or other reasons that may cause the position to be open. The near-term and long-term time lines may range from one year to five years in order to keep the administrative process current and up to date. Typically, the Human Resources Department and select members of senior management are involved in the administration of this important planning process. Additionally, the Succession Planning Administrative Process is linked to the organization's near-term and long- term strategic planning goals that embrace the need to plan for staffing key positions within the organization in order to run the business efficiently.

Depending on the position that the senior management team may take regarding the management, manpower, succession, planning, this program may or may not be confidential. If it is confidential, the employees who have been identified as high potentials will not be told that they are being considered for greater responsibility. If the program is not confidential, then the employees can be communicated with and told that they have been identified as high potentials. Senior management must decide what course they need to take to insure this program will be effective.

Chapter 7

Orientation and Training for New Hires

When a new hire enters the organization, it is critically important that the person be thoroughly oriented and trained. This must be done in order for the new hire to be productive and successful.

The areas of orientation and training should include the following:

Introduction to the Vision and Mission Statements (if available); assessment and overview of the workplace culture, the employee handbook, services, and/or products offered by the organization, relevant policies and procedures, a definitive overview of employee benefits offered by the company, and insight into who the customers are with regard to the products or services offered by the company.

Providing this kind of training and orientation for all new hires establishes an important knowledge base for them.

It is critically important, practical, and logical to provide this kind of orientation and training for *all* new hires. Scheduling this important process on a timely basis will help to ensure all new hires will have the knowledge they need to feel comfortable and to begin to make a contribution to the organization. These are the resources they will need to ensure they won't have a false start to their new position.

Chapter 8

Organizational Development Employee Training

T he training and development, or Human Resource development, has grown significantly at a tremendous rate for many years and continues to grow at a very rapid pace. This growth has been seen in all major organizations and various types of businesses, nationally and internationally because it makes sense to train and retrain employees at all levels within the organization. The biggest blockage may be affordability as a result of financial goals not being met. If an organization meets the needs of the employees, the employees will meet the needs and goals of the organization.

When designing and planning an employee training program, there are a number of planning components that need to be discussed prior to implementation. The following ideas should be considered prior to the finalization of a schedule: In many organizations, the training of employees is often referenced within the organization's Mission Statement and Annual

Operating Plan. Also, continuous learning in any organization is critically important. A well-planned training program will give employees a greater sense of self-worth, increase productivity, create a more positive attitude, and increase employees' self-esteem.

Once it has been determined that training programs are necessary, definitive training goals should be established. It isn't sufficient to say, "We want to improve the employees' knowledge, skills, attitudes, or behavior." What is important is to clarify what is to change specifically, why the changes are necessary, and by department, if appropriate. Also when planning an annual training program, timelines should be established for each training topic. This is important to ensure the training objectives are met and to avoid a false start.

The initial process should include the following:

- What training will be conducted, where, and when
- Who will facilitate the training
- Why the training is important and what the expected outcomes would be

Lastly, a letter to all employees introducing the training. The letter should be sent by the most senior manager (general manager, chief executive officer [CEO], president, etc.). The contents of the letter should clearly reference

the purpose of all future training programs and items one through three mentioned above.

An employee training program can be a significant learning experience. Ideally, a training program will have a permanent change in the employees' improved job performance. Therefore, training involves changing skills, knowledge, attitudes, or behavior.

The outcome of a well-planned training program may mean changing what employees know, the manner in which they perform, and their attitude toward their responsibilities and the organization.

It has been suggested that U.S. business firms spend billions of dollars each year on training programs to improve employee performance. Various forms of instruction revolve around formal lecture courses and seminars. This approach will help employees at all levels to acquire relevant knowledge that can be used sufficiently within their current positions.

Various organizations will contract with consulting firms to plan and conduct their training programs. Leadership will play a critical role in the planning and implementation of an organizational training program. In this regard, without a strong and committed, pro-active leadership throughout the organization, it would be difficult for the organization to continue to become a learning environment.

The culture of the organization is an important component if it is to become a learning environment. If a learning environment within the organization is to progress, everyone will need to agree on a shared vision with regard to training for all employees. Learning will not take place without new and well-planned information. It will be the organization that values continuous learning and strongly believes positives outcomes can be derived from this shared vision of well-coordinated training programs.

All training and development that is planned in an organization, ideally, should be cost effective. The benefits that could be gained must outweigh the various costs of training.

The intervention of organizational development and training will often produce positive change results. One of the most important outcomes could create openness and trust among co-workers and more respect for each other.

When a shared vision for training is discussed and accepted by the senior management members, primarily the CEO and Human Resources management representatives, the process in which to schedule and conduct the employee training will become time sensitive and cost effective. Their support will become critically important. Without it, the training becomes a waste of time and resources if it is not supported by those implementing it.

In a learning organization, all members take an active role in identifying and addressing performance-related concerns. This will be accomplished by sharing and applying newly acquired knowledge when and where needed.

The implementation of an employee training program will help the organization to shape its own future. These efforts can embrace a new and real voyage of discovery to improve employee performance and productivity.

Thousands of organizations are now engaged in planning and implementing training programs. Training continues to be a powerful tool. It is one of the most important ways in which to translate learning and knowledge into skills and action. Employee training will continue to be the interchange between purposeful information and ideas.

There are many reasons to help an organization to become high-performing through a well-planned training program. It is also important to remember that one of the outcomes of effective training will be stronger cohesion, enthusiastic teams, and outstanding performance that can be related to the bottom line of any organization.

Providing leadership through partnership and training will bring mental nutrition to employees. This chapter only represents a number of basic planning components when planning the implementation of employee training. Ultimately, training programs will be most effective if senior management utilizes their own observations and knowledge to include prior performance reviews of the employees associated with their business to conduct meaningful and relevant training programs.

Chapter 9

The Employee Performance Review Process

The administration of the Employee Performance Review Process is by far one of the most important responsibilities a manager has. This is an excellent opportunity for the manager to schedule a time for meeting with subordinates to discuss in detail their overall performance. In small and large organizations every employee is subject to a periodic performance appraisal. As is true of other aspects of development, the primary purpose of these appraisals has shifted in recent years. Originally it was a device to provide guidance to management in selecting employees for promotion or salary increases. Appraisals are now also used for coaching employees to improve their performance. An effective performance-appraisal program provides management with a rational basis for determining who should be promoted or receive salary increases.

The question emerges: why are such a high percentage of the performance review sessions done so poorly? Listed below are some the reasons why this happens so frequently:

- Lack of commitment
- Lack of planning
- Lack of an effective administrative system to insure the process begins on the scheduled date in which the employee is due to have the review
- Human Resources doesn't provide the leadership and influence necessary to avoid this problem from initially occurring

It would be critically important for an organization to insure that all the management people who have this kind of responsibility receive this training.

When scheduling and conducting an employee review session it is extremely important that the manager who is responsible for the performance review interview should be well prepared. The preparation should include a thorough review of the employee's file and past performance in addition to scheduling the interview a week in advance with the employee. The last important point is to ensure that the environment in which the performance review session is conducted will be professional, friendly, and without interruption.

When the Employee Performance Review is conducted professionally and effectively the results will be very positive. The employee being reviewed when the review is conducted in this manner will be made to feel important and the individual's self-esteem and productivity will increase significantly.

One of the most important responsibilities a leader has is to give feedback on performance to employees.

Chapter 10

Employee Morale is Critically Important

LEADERSHIP CIRCLE OF INFLUENCE

The morale of all employees in an organization is extremely important! A popular question constantly being asked by so many leaders is, "How do we accomplish this on a continuous basis?" This should always be a concern of management team members who are there to provide pro-active leadership to all employees. Some of the questions may be the following:

- How do we measure morale?
- How will low morale affect the motivation of employees?
- Will low morale have an affect on employee turnover?
- Will low morale have an affect on productivity?

In order to answer these questions completely, senior management needs to address employees' concerns. Additionally, there is a relationship between low morale, low self-esteem, and motivation. If morale is high then self-esteem, motivation, and productivity will be measurably high. So how is this accomplished in a way that is time sensitive and cost effective? There are a number of ways linked to leadership that this could be implemented.

This approach is also an important key to teamwork. Relevant knowledge should precede important decisions and actions. Another way to state it is: "Leadership through Partnership." These ideas in part are ways to avoid stagnation. One can't steer an ocean liner with a canoe paddle.

The following information on employee morale is based upon empirical data. If leadership is sincerely concerned about employee morale, there are action item steps that can be taken to address this concern. They are the following:

Supervisors and managers should be trained to be familiar with the topics of leadership, effective communications, how to conduct a meeting, motivation theories, how to conduct an employee performance review, the importance of an open door policy whereby employees feel comfortable speaking to their supervisor in confidence, and the importance of conducting an employee climate survey. If these topics are assimilated into the culture, there is a very high probability that morale will continually be high. The key link is to provide training programs that address this important concern on a continuous basis.

Another word for climate survey is an Employee Attitude Survey, which addresses the same purpose—to assess how employees feel about working for the organization. This process embraces facts and statistics to measure all areas of the working environment. Once this information is compiled and reviewed by responsible management, then actions items are put into place to address these concerns.

The worst thing that management can do is to make the decision to conduct an Employee Attitude Survey and then do nothing to address concerns expressed by the employees. This would clearly send a signal that management doesn't actually care what employees think about their work environment. Also, this would be a serious loss of credibility for senior management. It would be very difficult for management to recover from this loss of credibility.

Creating and cultivating a positive work environment will improve employee morale and productivity.

Chapter 11

The Importance of Teamwork

TEAMWORK AND TEAM BUILDING IS A PROCESS OF DISTRIBUTING LEADERSHIP

I n this segment of the Leadership Pocket Guide I will address the importance of teamwork and support the beginning of the contents with a brief definition of this significant part of leadership.

A team is a responsible group of employees who meet regularly to identify problems related to the organization and who work together openly to solve problems. Problem solving is their highest priority in order to achieve the *necessary* results to address and improve the *desired* results. The desired effectiveness of an organization will be greatly influenced by the quality of cooperation among its groups and its individual members. The team-building techniques described in the Pocket Guide have already been used by many organizations. All who participate in team building must be prepared to open their mind to new ideas and experiences. They must have a sincere desire to address old issues and to build new relationships. These ideas and methods must be tried and tested repeatedly until the desired outcomes are achieved in order to establish world-class efficiency.

The following is a listing of characteristics of highly effective teams:

- Team members understand and support the leader's goals.
- The team has a genuine desire to work together in an effort to address and resolve problems.
- There is visible respect among team members.
- Team members constantly try to give breath and life to the organization's vision and mission statements.

Communications among team members is shared and purposeful in order to achieve the completion of the pre-established meeting agenda and to achieve the necessary results to address and resolve organizational operational concerns and problems. The team leader or department manager encourages cooperation and synergy among team members in an effort to insure respect and satisfaction among team members.

Within the team culture, problem-solving techniques are utilized in order to resolve conflict and to complete objectives and goals. Management teams are consistently encouraged to utilize their collective professional knowledge and wisdom to solve problems and plan for the future. When purposeful teams are formed they continually plan for the future quite often on a monthly, quarterly, semi-annually, and annual basis in order to assess the status of the business year to date. A strong and cohesive team has the desire and spirit to professionally resolve conflict and achieve the desired results to make important and significant contributions to the organization. Teamwork that results in continuous excellent performance will clearly have a positive impact on morale and can be measured at the financial bottom line.

The following is a list of what to look for when a team becomes visibly dysfunctional:

- The team avoids conflict and exhibits avoidance behavior.
- The same problems are repeated and nothing is accomplished.
- During scheduled team meetings, the agenda may not be followed, leading to frustration and criticism.
- If there is an established agenda, it may not be followed rendering the meeting a waste of time.
- The team leader loses control and various team members may dominate the meeting—participation becomes limited to only those few.
- A sense of responsibility and respect for other team members will become visibly absent.
- A sense of responsibility for others within the team may appear to be declining.
- Current efforts to try and create a positive environment by team members in which create and environment of cooperation will be reduced. Unrelated side conversations begin to take place during team meetings.

- The same few team members begin to dominate the meeting and do most of the talking.

Keep the momentum alive! The process of team building is a continuous learning process of taking action with an open mind and seeking better solutions for today's business challenges.

Develop good habits and make them your masters.

Chapter 12

Trust Deposits

T here cannot be effective and purposeful leadership without trust. Leaders must earn and maintain the trust of their employees throughout the organization from the senior management team to the first line supervisor. If the management team wants to have any degree of credibility, they must earn and maintain a high degree of trust.

In order to build continuous trust in the eyes of employees, role modeling is also an important component of leadership and trust. Employees hear what their leaders *say*, but they watch and observe what they *do*. This is a simplistic definition of Role Modeling. Based upon empirical data from a number of business segments where there is measurable trust in a department or organization, the motivation among employees will be consistently high. If trust is lacking, the opposite effect will be very visible.

There will always be a certain percentage of employees in every organization who will do only what is required of them—the very minimum to insure they retain their job—and no more. This kind of behavior will continue until there is a change in the management of the department. The symptoms that will most commonly emerge are low morale, attrition, possibly a decrease in the quality of the product or service, and gossip. There is a duality between high self-esteem among employees and motivation. Conversely, when the self-esteem among various employees is low, then productivity and motivation will also be low. If the needs of the employees are met, then the needs or requirements of the department or organization will be met. Pro- active Leadership is an important choice and necessity. It is vital for the leaders to create continuous levels of high performance. This can only be accomplished if there is a culture of trust. Within the definition of "Leadership," every minute counts as managers make every effort to fulfill their important role as leaders. Senior management, of all leadership segments, has a responsibility to review the leadership methods to insure that they are being applied pro-actively and effectively. This is a basic common-sense approach to ensure that the objectives they are responsible for are met. People aspire to identify with organizations that they can respect.

There is clearly a relatedness between learning, leading, and trust.

Chapter 13

Conflicts: Costly If Not Addressed

There is a high probability that within various cultures or departments there will be conflicts among department managers and/or employees within an organization.

The very best way to begin to address this issue and to prepare employees with the basics on how to address conflict is through training. Typically, the various kinds of conflict that are normally linked to various business segments usually take place within some aspect of the operational areas of a business. When this takes place, employees become frustrated, uncertain, and relationships become strained if not broken.

Productivity may suffer, goals are not met, and ultimately customers may become dissatisfied with the product or service. As an important point of reference, a typical dissatisfied customer may tell eight to ten people or more about the problem they experienced. On the average, it may take ten to fourteen positive service incidents to make up for one problem incident.

When this happens, there could be a loss of customers and revenue; no organization can afford this problematic outcome.

Taking time to train employees on the methods to resolve conflict is critically important. This process starts with leadership, effective communication, and commitment. The training approach may be scheduled training with a professional facilitator, or it may be conducted by a department manager or by way of an informal meeting by the department manager.

Where there is an issue or disagreement, employees need to focus on the issue and not point fingers at each other. Re-directing fault will only enhance the issue and not resolve the problem. If there is commitment to resolve the conflict, then quality communication, positive attitude, fact finding, and a sincere desire to resolve the problem will be necessary. If these components are visible and present in an environment of harmony and not "departmental fences" the conflict will be resolved to everyone's satisfaction. Resolving conflict requires believability, commitment, and situational leadership.

Chapter 14

Attitude Is Everything

Webster's Dictionary defines attitude as: "A mental position with regard to a fact or state; a position assumed for a specific purpose; a feeling of emotion toward a fact or state." The importance of this definition is for the purpose of awareness and understanding of what attitude means and the negative or positive affect on an employee's performance.

Attitude is extremely important in the sense of how one may approach one's job on a daily basis. It doesn't matter what one's position may be in the organization. What does matter is that each employee who is a member of a department or team tries to develop and maintain a positive attitude. Having a positive attitude can be contagious.

Also important is that the manager of a department or team know each member and to keep them focused and motivated. This can only be done if the manager is familiar with the various behavioral patterns of each team member. Knowing and understanding each individual and having some insight into each one's personality will allow the leader to remove any problems within the department. Leaders are defined by their good intentions and good deeds. Keeping each of the department members motivated and understanding their needs will result in synergy for the team, ensuring compatibility and meeting or exceeding department goals.

Pro-active leadership needs to be continuous for the purpose of developing people and teams. This also involves continuous, quality communication every day. Without quality communication, leadership is incomplete.

It is always important to be generous with praise for a job well done.

Chapter 15

Optimizing Communication and Feedback

C lear Communications Associated with Expectations Will Empower Subordinates Communication is defined as a person sending a message to another individual for the purpose of evoking a response. There is a sender, a receiver, and a message that may be verbal, nonverbal, or behavioral. Full communication is achieved when the receiver understands the full meaning of the message as it was intended by the sender. This must include not only the content, as carried by the words, or special meaning that may have influenced the selection of the words used in order for the message to be effective. The definition of communication involves at least two individuals—the sender of information and the receiver of the message. The receiver receives the sender's message and responds to the information and sends the sender a verbal or nonverbal message in order for the message to be completed. This process may include written memo messages, e-mail, verbal communication, and any information that may take place in various meetings.

Effective leadership is the attainment of organizational goals in an effective and efficient manner through planning, organizing, and controlling organizational resources. This approach to managing cannot be done without purposeful, effective, and continuous communication. One of the most important building blocks for team performance is open communication. All members of the team are encouraged to participate in discussions involved in the decision-making process that may involve roles and responsibilities, operating procedures, and other leadership decisions.

Without effective communication, pro-active leadership will be reduced and the results will be costly waste to the organization.

Organizational Leadership Communication Model

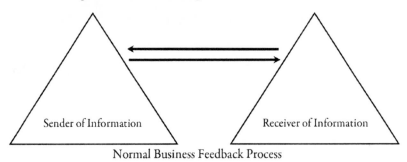

Normal Business Feedback Process

- Both parties may need to adjust/revise information in order to ensure understanding.

- Without effective communications, pro-active leadership will be reduced and the results will be costly waste to the organization.

Figure 15.1

Chapter 16

Organizational Change

To survive and succeed, every organization will have to turn itself into a change agent. The most effective way to manage change successfully is to create it. This is especially so in large-scale organizational changes involving new technologies, new strategies, e-business, restructuring, mergers, acquisitions, and globalization.

When and where appropriate, individual managers and supervisors should recommend and make changes in an effort to improve organizational effectiveness. By definition, this may also be called situational leadership. Examples may include employee morale, a safety program, quality programs, ways in which to save the organization money, how to conduct an effective and productive meeting, and so on. Providing leadership is the role of all individuals who have managerial responsibility. They are clearly the underpinnings of the organization. It isn't how smart a leader is that is important. What is important is how leaders use their intelligence.

Understanding what the organization requires from it's leadership team to accomplish continuous success will always be important. Leaders should not need permission to provide situational leadership when and where needed. Pro-active Leadership should always be cultivated and encouraged, not a "pushership" style of leadership or management by fear. This doesn't mean doing away with discipline. If an employee should be disciplined for poor performance or absenteeism or some other form of unacceptable behavior, discipline should be administered. Administration of the Employee Discipline Policy ideally should be referenced in the Employee Handbook. If warranted, progressive discipline should be applied as fairly as possible.

When management recognizes the need for a change of any kind, the management team should consider how to enable the change for the planned changes to be effective. This requires the organized abandonment of things that have been shown to be unsuccessful. In this regard, how the changes will be implemented is extremely important. Other realistic options should also be considered. For example, who will introduce and begin the initiation of the planned changes? What employee group(s) will be affected? What are the various time lines in which to complete the changes? How will this information be communicated to those affected? What is the anticipated reaction to the changes once announced? Will employee morale and productivity be affected? These are the many questions that should be addressed and discussed when planning important changes.

One of the most important strategic questions that should be thoroughly discussed is how will the information be communicated to employees? What communication channels will be used? The following ideas could be considered when planning changes: 1) Departmental meetings; 2) An employee newsletter; 3) Letters to the homes of all of the employees affected, signed by the president or general manager, whatever is appropriate; 4) Make it known that an "open door policy" is in effect for anyone wishing to have his or her questions answered. If these strategic options are considered, adversity to change should be minimal. Senior Management should also try to anticipate how the employees may react to the changes. Will employee morale and productivity be affected? Will turnover be affected? How will the customer base be affected? It is recommended that when changes are announced that continuous communication with the employees be utilized to insure that they understand the need for the changes.

When feasible, leaders should schedule and conduct a "state of the business" meeting with employees.

Chapter 17

How to Conduct an Effective, Useful, and Purposeful Meeting

When planning to conduct a scheduled meeting, the following administrative steps should be adhered to by the person conducting the meeting and the attending participants.

Every meeting should have a Leader. He or she may go under the name of chairperson, ranking executive, manager, chief executive officer or supervisor. The final outcome of any meeting hinges on this individual's leadership ability.

These are the steps to conduct a meeting:

- Announce the meeting seven to ten days in advance.
- The advanced announcement should be communicated in such a way that would be normal to the culture (e.g., e-mail, memo).
- Start and end the meeting on time without exception.
- Consider starting with a short ice-breaker in order to get the attendees to feel comfortable with each other and to prepare for the agenda.

- The person chairing the meeting should try to involve all the persons in attendance. This may require training to better understand group dynamics.
- If action items are assigned to various participants, it is important to establish a date for completion.
- If the existing culture is accustomed to having Minutes recorded for future reference and filing, this should be included.

The following is a listing of various symptoms of communication problems that may occur:

- Confusion in the implementation of decisions.
- An increase in subordinated demands for personal contact.
- A need to repeat communication at a later time.
- Unaccountable increases in mistakes.
- An increase in the general anxiety level.
- Rumors and increased activity of the employee "grapevine."
- A subordinate who makes frequent demands on the manager for reassurance to insure that the message being received and heard is correct.

The Six Communication Skills that most employees use are the following:

1. Writing
2. Speaking
3. Listening
4. Reading

5. E-mail

6. Texting

Managers who are responsible for effective organizational communications should consider doing the following to improve communication within the organization:

- Hold regular group meetings.
- Communicate in language employees can understand.
- Don't always depend on the written word alone.
- Have frequent, direct face-to-face contact with employees.
- Consider your employees your most valuable resource.
- Consider holding departmental meetings with all employees.
- Senior Management should hold "state of the business" meetings with all employees, annually or every six months.

It is important to note that "uncertainty" is clearly the opposite of information. Full Communication is achieved when the receiver understands the full meaning of the message as it was intended by the sender. This must include not only the content, as carried by the words, but also special meanings that may have a purpose related to the words used to send the message to insure complete understanding.

Communication is one of the most important elements of good leadership, yet it is one of the least used and understood. Don't manage by "muzzling employees."

The absence of quality communication will cause leadership to be incomplete.

Chapter 18

Team or Group Brainstorming

The team or group brainstorming process is often used not only as a meeting "ice breaker" but also as a purposeful technique designed to generate a large number of ideas through interaction among group members or team members. As an important part of this administrative process, the facilitator has the responsibility of encouraging teamwork and creativity. The ideal outcomes that may result from this process are the following:

- The topic or problem is clarified by the participating members.
- Ideas are never criticized.
- All ideas are recorded.
- The idea list is narrowed down in an effort to arrive at closure.
- A detailed discussion should be the next step to discuss the practicality and cost of the various ideas.

- Once this is completed, one idea should be selected and discussed for evaluation and implementation.

Lastly, it is important to emphasize that in order for this process to be useful and effective, the facilitator and participating members must be trained in basic components of the brainstorming process. Unless there is commitment to accomplish this kind of training, the outcome may be ineffective or even a waste of time.

For an example of a Brainstorming Activity Sheet, please refer to page 153.

Chapter 19

Leadership Fundamentals

Trust is vital for all leaders to have.
A leader should be a good teacher and communicator.
A leader should be a problem solver.
A leader must know how to manage time well
and use it effectively.
A leader must have technical competence in order
to effectively lead teams within
the organization and accomplish the necessary goals.
Leaders must know the importance of providing vision
and mission for the organization.
It is important that leaders know how to conduct effective
and productive meetings
in order to complete the agenda in a timely fashion. Leaders
must be approachable for all subordinates and managers.
Leaders should have a sense of humor.
Leaders should be reliable.
Leaders should display a high level of integrity at all times.

A leader must understand the importance and knowledge of how to motivate employees.
A leader should be open minded and try to see the merit of other ideas, even if they conflict with his or her own.
Leaders freely give positive and helpful feedback to subordinates.
Leaders encourage excellent performance and give credit where it is due. When mistakes are made within the department, leaders know how to become effective coaches to assist subordinates to learn from their mistakes
Leaders continuously establish departmental and individual objectives to insure the mission of the department is successfully met.
A leader's communication is personalized so each employee knows there is an interest in him or her.
A leader is continuously seeking new procedures in an effort to improve the overall performance of the organization.
A leader knows the importance of asking employees for advice or suggestions about
how to improve a process or procedure
or how to address problems.

Nothing in the world will take the place of continuous persistence in order to have positive outcomes.

Chapter 20

Why Do People Work In the World?

Why do people work in the world? People need to work in the world to feel like they have purpose in their lives. Ever since the beginning of time, mankind had a purpose—to survive. In the very beginning it was food, water, and shelter. As primitive as it may have been, they did survive. As time went on, they discovered fire and began to heavily depend upon it for continuous survival.

As the centuries passed, people became extremely advanced in the world within different cultures. New discoveries were made. Advanced technologies through scientific research were also discovered. However, the need to survive in addition to finding continuous ways to find happiness also continued.

So, once again why do people work? Why do the majority of people need a purpose in their lives?

All people need to feel purposeful. Without a sense of "belonging" or that they are necessary, they feel superfluous and this clearly effects their attitude and self- esteem. Within the definition of leadership, attitude is everything. Attitude is the very foundation of a leader's thought process. A leader, by definition, in business can be a group leader, supervisor, manager, vice-president, general manager, chief executive officer, or president. Within the individual roles there should be a positive attitude in which to inspire, communicate, and lead people. The responsibility of leading is relevant to predet ermined goals to accomplish something, to be productive in some way, whether large or small.

These statements are common sense for anyone who is responsible for leading people. If agreement is reached upon reading this information, the question continues to be asked: why then is leadership and maintaining a positive attitude so difficult? Could it be a lack of training? Is it possible the wrong people are in the wrong positions? Is it possible the environment in which various people are working is so negative that they can't make a difference no matter what they may try to do? Perhaps it is some of each of these reasons. The twenty-first century is about change and intervention. To be successful, leaders must have the necessary skill and confidence to lead.

Chapter 21

Depository of Truth

S everal of the most critical seeds of leadership to cultivate is trust and integrity. If leaders are to initiate credibility and build credibility within their departments, organizations, and corporations, pure and simple, they must be trusted. Trust and integrity are the key underpinnings people rely upon. Without these two components, motivation will be affected, productivity will be affected, communications will be affected and, in time, the lack of these two seeds could affect employee turnover. Employees may request transfers to other departments within the organization or leave for other positions with other organizations.

Leaders today are partially defined by their ability to establish and build trust and integrity. The question that may be asked upon the completion of reading this overview is how can this be accomplished? Firstly, it is believability, trust and integrity that are important characteristics that are needed in a leader's responsibility. Once this is accepted, the next steps may involve training that will help to document and cultivate the importance of these characteristics. Secondly, of course, would be to implement these important values when leading teams. Once implemented, results in teamwork, productivity, morale, quality, and turnover will be very positive.

Chapter 22

The Purpose of Organizational Health

The following information is a definitive listing of components that measure the culture of an organization and "Organizational Health." Most organizations only take advantage of a very small percentage of the knowledge, experience, training, and education that is available to them from their existing workforce. This is truly unfortunate! If the right environment is created by senior management—senior management must always set the example—employees would be encouraged to share their ideas throughout the organization. Very few organizations invest enough of their time, energy, and planning to create such an environment.

These, in my view, are the characteristics of pro-active, great leaders. This approach and overall process to teamwork and building teams brings a significant advantage to building effective teams throughout the organization. To unlock employees' hidden talents and potential, senior management must decide that this approach would be useful to be a part of their strategic plans.

One way in which an organization may be able to reduce employees' mistrust of management is to get them involved in the decision-making process. By allowing employees to become involved, leaders will be able to improve their understanding of employees' needs and problems. This approach will also encourage employees to seek new ideas to existing problems, which will help leaders improve many of their systems and policies. Employee involvement is a management philosophy and process that encourages, allows, or requires employees to become involved in some aspects of the management decision process. This approach, if administered effectively, helps management develop more innovative solutions to existing problems, which could also mean cost saving, improvement in quality, increased morale, and so on.

In this author's view, there is no one particular employee involvement program that will satisfy all of the organization's needs. The obvious reason for this is that each organization is uniquely different. If and when those in senior management decide to begin an employee involvement program, they need to clearly decide which type of program will help them to achieve their near-term and long-term strategic plans and which employees will be selected to participate. Leadership concepts are easy to create and to implement; however, they are very difficult and complicated to administer. A pro-active leader must have a thorough understanding of these concepts; the employees that he or she manages, what cause and effect the concepts may have on a team, and ways in which to measure the results once implemented.

At the center of every culture are visions of the future and values that guide behavior within an organization. Also, within every culture are fundamental elements such as an organizational structure, systems, skills, management styles, and values that support the organization's vision and mission. These fundamental elements are the building blocks that will help shape or re-shape the organization's culture and establish a degree of cohesion among departments and the various teams within each of the departments.

If this kind of major change in the culture is to be successful, the management and the employees need to be totally committed at the very beginning of such a program. This would require a major change in the way they would traditionally conduct business. Without this degree of commitment, employees may view management as insincere and might not support these new objectives.

At the very beginning of such a change, there must be clear and purposeful communication to all employees followed by orientation and training for those who will be involved in the program. Lastly, senior management must provide the necessary resources, time, and budgeted money. This may include allowing employees time away from their work areas to participate in training sessions and other necessary program components. Some serious consideration should also be given to some type of a cost effective reward system.

Leadership is like a house, something
always needs to be fixed.

Chapter 23

Sharing Leadership

LEADERSHIP WITHOUT FENCES

E ffective Leadership involves sharing important responsibilities with other employees who have expressed a desire to broaden their scope of responsibility and who may have the basic skills needed to lead. It is to the benefit of leaders and team members to share portions of the leadership role. This will, in turn, build self- confidence in team members and expand their capabilities. It will also give the leader more confidence in the abilities of the team when the leader must be absent so that the day-to-day objectives are successfully met or even, in some cases, exceeded.

While there are various ways to exercise leadership, one of the goals of any leader should be to share the skill he or she possesses with various team members. This would help to strengthen the team. This goal would embrace the idea that an effective leader must be willing to also be a teacher.

To teach implies that one is willing to make an effort to pass one's own knowledge on to others. When this is done successfully, the self-esteem of those being taught will increase significantly. This in itself will have very positive benefits for high morale, high productivity, a more cohesive team, goals being met, and so on.

Leadership is a very complex subject. The speed at which knowledge is accessible in the twenty-first century continues to astound everyone. But this knowledge is one of the key elements to success for both leaders and employees and enables them to make a valuable contribution to the organization. A learning organization is a journey with no end in sight. Leaders should continually assess their vision and mission statements and modify them when appropriate and necessary to remain competitive in this ever-changing world. Sharing the vision and mission will clearly create a sense of pride and purpose with all employees. In today's ever-changing, fast paced environment, successful leaders need to realize that the financial success of their organization involves a careful balance of the technological advances of domestic and global business and the complex understanding that motivates employees. Leaders also need to understand the importance of giving life to their vision and mission statements to insure they will have meaning that will support the goals of the organization through their teams.

Chapter 24

Employee Counseling

The counseling process that may be needed to address a team-based environment is often mistaken for criticism unless it is fully understood. Effective leaders will dispel this fear once they have demonstrated to team members that their intent is to help them improve in areas of performance that require behavioral change. Counseling will continue to be a process to help managers solve operational problems, if they should emerge. If done professionally and effectively by a trained manager, this approach will help establish an environment that will be non- threatening to employees. It reassures them that the process is needed to improve performance. It will also help each member of the team to reach his or her full potential.

Upon concluding this topic on counseling, it is important that the department leader must first try to completely understand the situation. Leaders must listen carefully, then summarize, and verify facts completely to determine the root cause of the problem. Once this is completed, the counselor meets with the individual or group to discuss the findings and determine the best solution to correct the problem.

The counselor's role is to give encouragement and advice in an effort to make the team more cohesive and work together to address the performance issues. A "cup" of this kind of leadership helps improve employee behavior, change a negative attitude, improve morale, increase productivity, and reduce employee turnover, bringing a win-win end result.

I am a realist, however, and managers can't win them all. As I often say, perfect intentions by imperfect people. Managers at all levels do the best they can with the facts they have, within the policies of the organization. They make every effort to be consistent, treat employees with dignity and fairness and, at the same time, run the business they are responsible for. This process will help the team or department to become more cohesive.

Chapter 25

The Clarity of Leadership

COMMON ELEMENTS

C learly there are a number of common leadership elements that each manager would need for them to develop as an effective manager. Leadership is a major part of any business. The importance of leadership has been recognized since the very early times. Effective leadership is the major key that can mean the difference between the success and failure of any business. Pro-active leadership is the influencing of others within a department to work willingly toward successfully achieving pre-determined objectives. Defining the elements of leadership related to determining the kind of leadership style is critically important to insure the leader will be the appropriate choice for many operational and strategic reasons.

Important choices made in selecting the right leader will affect the organizational health of a department, company, or a senior management position at the corporate level. These staffing choices will assist in the transformation of unhealthy organizations into healthy ones. The key result of this transformation will be very cohesive teams. This is also a way to intellectualize the various components of the culture without bureaucratizing it through the various elements of pro-active leadership. This process could also result in the re-birth of leadership by implementing these various steps to create a healthy organization and cohesive teams throughout. This information is only one of the many "Prescriptions for Leadership." Albert Einstein once said, "No new problem can be solved by the same consciousness that created it. We need to see the world anew."

Please reference the Leadership Summary Overview on page 92 and 93 for more examples of common leadership elements.

Leadership Summary Overview

The following is a list of attributes and activities that summarize the activities of successful leadership:

- Vision – Mission
- Trust – Honesty – Integrity – Honor
- Building Teams – Teamwork
- Goals and Objectives
- Global Focus
- Morals – Ethics
- Communication – Written, Verbal, Non-Verbal
- Leadership Thinking Skills – Be Proactive

- Customer Service Orientation
- Conducting Effective Meetings
- Coaching – Counseling
- Training – Learning Organization
- Employee Involvement
- Implementing Change
- Effective Recruiting
- Open Door Policy
- Respect for Others
- Synergy
- Physical Vitality and Stamina
- Capacity to Motivate
- Conflict Resolution Skills
- Problem-solving Process Skills
- Strategic Thinking and Planning Near-term and Long-term
- Financial Success
- Intellectual Energy and Curiosity
- Situational Leadership Skills
- Building Organizational Harmony
- Social Skills – Sense of Humor
- Emotional Intelligence

Giving leadership life and meaning.

Chapter 26

Leadership Thinking Skills

ARTICULATING A
CLEAR SENSE OF PURPOSE

B eing a leader requires more than possessing knowledge about leadership. The leader also needs to have leadership thinking skills. In an effort to thoroughly assess the overall performance of a team within a department or organization, leaders must familiarize themselves with the day-to-day operations of the business to determine which of the objectives and or strategies have been met and which of the objectives have not been met and why. This attention to detail and overall approach is a *must* if the organizational objectives are going to be successfully met. Asking why the team has not met its goals or objectives should lead to identifying what has led to the failure of the team.

The leader may be faced with two possibilities: was it a human error or possibly an equipment problem that caused the team to miss a date(s) for completion? Additionally, the leader should be looking for cause and effect chronological events that may be a significant part of the root cause of the problem.

At this point in the fact finding stage, the leader and the team must decide what should be done to address the problem and decide on a realistic and time-sensitive plan of action. This could involve restructuring the team by replacing some of the members who are not committed to the objectives of the group or adding new team members. This approach may also involve consulting with different departments in an effort to determine more of the facts that may have had a negative impact on the teams' efforts. The leader must find the right solution (situational leadership) to correct the problem in order for the team to the meet its objectives.

Leaders should always strive to create
camaraderie among employees.

Chapter 27

Role Modeling

Role Modeling is a very important part of leadership today in all business segments. Setting an example is one of the most important leadership skills a leader needs to possess. As the expression goes "we hear what leaders say, but we watch what they do." Modeling is one of the most effective ways to show others the proper way in which to conduct themselves. In business, it is usually not just what leaders say, but what he or she does that will influence and shape employees' behavior.

Leaders will display a value system and belief in their style of leadership that will be visible to the employees in a group, department, or team. These leadership elements will have an influence on the team members' trust of their leader and their ability to perform cohesively and meet the predetermined objectives successfully as a team. Leaders will also instill personal values that are visible to the team and that are consistent with building self-confidence in team members, sharing of authority, and ensuring the team has the tools and information needed to perform effectively and successfully.

This is clearly the real world of business because leadership today in the modern world is not a simple activity—it is much more complex than just telling people what to do. The leader develops and communicates a shared vision and mission of the future among the team members. This cannot be accomplished without trust. There is a duality between trust and role modeling. One cannot exist without the other. This is an important underpinning in order for the work environment to be positive and the employees to be motivated.

It is extremely important that all leaders lead by example
if they are to influence others.

Chapter 28

Leadership and Planning

The importance of planning is necessary at all levels in an organization. Planning is an essential element of leadership in all segments of business involving leaders and team members. The planning process is essential if the various teams are going to achieve the goals and objectives that have been established within each of their departments.

Many organizations have found it necessary and useful to establish in writing, one-year plans, three-year plans, and five-year plans. These plans also encompass the various strategies to include resources, time lines, goals, and objectives that are in writing and, if achieved, what the desired result will be. When established in writing, these plans will provide direction, become time sensitive and include a date for completion, and will be enhanced by a cohesive team in order to be successful. The leader will be accountable for the implementation and administration of the various plans. In this regard it is very common for organizations to have weekly or monthly staff meetings to discuss progress.

Depending on the organizational structure, the senior management members report to a general manager, chief executive officer, or president. The reporting structure of the senior management staff could involve various departments such as marketing, human resources, finance, engineering, manufacturing, research and development, and international. This would be a high-technology, manufacturing organization.

Within the hospitality business—specifically hotels—the senior management staff, also known as the executive committee, would be: marketing, finance, rooms, food and beverage, human resources, and engineering. The leaders in those positions report to a general manager of the hotel.

In the health care industry, the senior management staff includes the following: nursing, finance, human resources, radiology, engineering, marketing, patient relations, and a senior medical staff member. These are the senior management team members that provide the leadership, guidance, and overall direction for each of these industries. They steer the ship, so to speak, using a predetermined strategic compass that encompasses the vision and mission statements.

During senior management staff meetings the agenda would essentially require that the members be prepared to discuss the progress of their goals and objectives or the overall status of each of their departments. This may be done using PowerPoint, overhead transparencies, flip charts, or conversation around a board table. Whatever the method used, this process will give an update on the goals and objectives and would also give other members of the senior management team the opportunity to be updated and to ask questions of each presenter.

If the process is communicated and effectively administered, each member of the senior management team will make a contribution that he or she is responsible for what will continually support the goals and objectives of the organization. Typically, at the beginning of a new business year—fiscal or calendar—each of the senior management team would submit a plan or a white paper that specifically references what he or she plans to accomplish during the next twelve months. This report is then submitted to the person to whom she or he reports—president, general manager, chief executive officer, hospital administrator, and so on.

Once these plans are approved in writing, they are then communicated to all of the members of each discipline. This process and overall relationship among the senior management team members is critical to the organization's success. They must be committed to work well together, taking ownership for their goals and objectives and the position they hold in the organization. Owners depict a high degree of responsibility for their part of the operation. Leadership through partnership with each of the senior management team members, direct reports, and the employees in each of these departments will enable the organization to be successful.

A visionary leader will need to adapt plans to unexpected changes to avoid problematic outcomes.

Chapter 29

Creating Balance in Your Life Between Work and Exercise

In order to create balance in your life between working and staying healthy, it is extremely important to have a schedule that includes some form of exercise. Many managers and employees spend a great deal of time at work.

The normal schedule for a full-time employee is 2,080 hours a year. That is a significant amount of time to spend at your place of employment. Although it is important to remain committed and focused on one's job, earning a living and displaying your commitment, it is also important to form good exercise habits. To provide effective leadership, managers need to seriously consider a way to maintain physical hardiness or increase physical strength.

Because a high percentage of managers are very busy people with their work, family, maintaining a home, perhaps traveling, it may be time to embrace the Time Management Concepts. These concepts help a great deal to plan the time needed to schedule some form of physical activity. The physical activity could include walking, riding a bike, swimming, rowing a boat, and so on.

During the last decade, research has supported the fact that exercise has the potential of reducing stress and tension. The medical community has also supported the fact that exercise is one of the best ways to effect good health. One of the advantages of some form of exercise is that it doesn't require more than twenty to thirty minutes a day. However, to be of any benefit, it must be scheduled on a regular basis. According to exercise physiologists, exercise tends to build a healthier self-concept. There is a high probability that people who exercise could feel better about themselves and may become more self-confident.

One of the keys to a regular exercise program is to choose something that you enjoy. In the beginning goals should be small and achievable. Consideration should be given to maintaining an exercise log or journal. Doing this provides detailed information about your exercise program and could help you stay motivated. It is also important to note the following: When changing your diet or beginning a new fitness program, it is advisable to seek medical advice from your physician, especially if you are currently taking any prescription medicines.

Leaders need to make time in their day for a period
of solitude.

Chapter 30

Emotional Intelligence and Leadership

Within the definition of proactive leadership today in the business world, leaders at all levels are faced with a large amount of information to make effective, professional decisions. These decisions will be reflective of their leadership and will have some affect on the scope of their responsibilities, which could have an affect on the organization. In this regard, they are dealing with complex information in an effort to run the business efficiently every day. This information typically encompasses the employees they supervise, customers, quality issues, production issues, cost of doing business, and other concerns. There will be times where more research is required on a given topic in order for the information to be complete.

For leaders to generate inspiration and motivation, they must have the desire, knowledge, and ability to provide leadership within their scope of responsibility in each of their respective departments. I strongly believe that organization-ally, this should start at the very top of the organization and be visible throughout the culture. Perhaps this would be viewed as role modeling throughout the organization, which is an important component of proactive leadership.

It is also important for leaders to understand the various behavior patterns of the employees they supervise, including their emotions, problems they may be experiencing on the job, and various needs the employees have. Leaders must get to know employees on an individual basis, not personally, but professionally. This is clearly a form of objective and construc-tive thinking that should be exercised throughout the organiza-tion. Leaders need to insure that they have all the necessary facts to make important decisions that may affect their depart-ment, the organization, or other employees. They must also follow the rules and regulations that may be established within the formal Employee Handbook. This analysis would support Emotional Intelligence and should be considered as a way to process the efficient running of the business and leadership. This approach is very relevant to modern day leadership.

To accept this approach and to consistently make it work, won't be easy. It will take a great deal of hard work through believability and persistence. The end result will be the accep-tance of this kind of leadership from the workforce, higher morale, improved quality and productivity, lower turnover, and much more efficiency throughout the organization over all. If this makes sense to those who read this portion of the Pocket Guide, then it should be tried and tested to determine if it will be useful for your department or organization. If this is to be considered, don't wait until conditions are perfect, they never will be. Managers can expect obstacles and difficulties and they should be solved as they arise. Ideas alone won't bring change and success to the organization. Ideas have value only when they are implemented, followed up, and when corrective action is taken when needed. Take the initiative and get started in an effort to improve the culture through this new process of leading. You will be happy that you did!

Chapter 31

Leadership Reborn

Restoring the Balance of Leadership

Acquiring knowledge is extremely important. How we use it is even more important. Understanding Emotional Intelligence can clearly be an advantage for managers when leading people, building teams, and working toward meeting organizational and departmental objectives. Having this knowledge is a critical skill necessary to be successful as a leader. The mind once expanded to dimensions of larger ideas and knowledge, never returns to its original size. In a way this is an approach to avoid mental sclerosis or hardening of the attitudes, a term referred to by Linda and Charlie Bloom in their blog, "Building Relationship Skills." This approach is also an important key to teamwork. Relevant knowledge should precede important decisions and actions. Perhaps another way to state it would be "Leadership through Partnership." These ideas, in part, are ways in which to avoid stagnation. One can't steer an ocean liner with a canoe paddle.

Develop good habits and make them your masters.

Chapter 32

The Uncertainty of Business

PRESCRIPTION FOR LEADERSHIP

If the unexpected should happen, which it frequently does in business, will your organization be ready? Will your senior managers know how to make important business decisions? Will the various departmental teams be prepared to resolve those issues they may be faced with? These are just a few questions that business leaders should ask themselves. If teams aren't trained to effectively address the uncertainty with regard to a variety of issues that need to be resolved, what needs to be done to make them ready? This, of course, involves being prepared with a strategic vision and mission. This is clearly the foundation of good leadership and not poor leadership. If an organization meets the needs of the people (employees), they will meet the needs of the business. Of course this knowledge must be known and understood by all the managers within the organizational structure before this important approach will do any good.

Conclusion

As we come to the end of the Pocket Guide, it is our hope that all readers will find the contents meaningful and useful. You must go forward as a learner if you are going forward as a leader. Wisdom is the continuous acquisition of knowledge, facts, and the desire to keep learning.

If the organization meets the needs of the employees, the employees will meet the needs of the organization. In the end it''s all about people.

Case Study Overview

Please note: All case studies were uniquely created and written to support the various chapters within the leadership book. All case studies are completely fictitious and were designed in their entirety by the author.

In the author's effort to create these hypothetical leadership cases, his many years of college and university teaching background was fully utilized. These cases are intended to supplement the conceptual material and to help readers to better understand the leadership process more completely.

These cases were also created to make the book more reader friendly, and to develop critical thinking skills.

Case Study A

HEALTH CARE ORGANIZATION

This case study involves a small hospital in the Northeastern part of the United States. The specifics are related to a vice president of Nursing and her specific style of leadership. To be more specific, her style of leadership was very auto-cratic, dictatorial, and controlling. She had earned quite a neg-ative reputation and was actually feared by the nursing staff at all levels. The president of the hospital had warned her on a number of occasions to change her approach when interacting with those in her department. The hospital was non-union and clearly tried to promote an open door policy to hear the con-cerns of all employees, including the nursing organization.

The Human Resources vice president (HRVP) had taken a pro-active approach for many years to insure that the hos-pital remained non-union in addition to making every effort to increase morale throughout the hospital. There were numerous occasions that required the HRVP to have discussions with the VP of Nursing to make her aware of concerns being expressed by various members of the nursing staff. After a period of time, the relationship between the HRVP and the VP of Nursing had become one of conflict and awkwardness. The VP of Nursing was essentially in denial and wasn't willing to make a genuine effort to change her leadership style. This, of course, was very problematic. The HRVP had created a file to document every meeting with the VP of Nursing.

The complaints and concerns continued for a long period of time and the morale of the nursing staff was at an all-time low. In an effort to keep the president of the hospital up to date, meetings were held periodically to brief him on the details of each meeting. The president was very concerned, but wasn't willing to take disciplinary action of any kind.

Morale was very low and rumors about needing a union to represent the nursing staff. This became a very serious concern of the president, members of the Board of Directors, and other members of management. Once a union campaign begins, the effort to insure that a business doesn't become unionized is mentally and physically difficult.

The key person to take this kind of lead is usually the HRVP, and he did. He had begun to schedule meetings with the nurse managers without the VP of Nursing present. This was a joint decision that was supported by the president of the hospital and the chairman of the board, and recommended by the HRVP. As the meetings were scheduled and held and chaired by the HRVP, the information had begun to be gathered and summarized for analysis and for the purpose of making a log-ical conclusion.

The findings clearly pointed to a lack of pro-active leadership by the VP of Nursing. Her pattern of behavior was very negative, demeaning, and showed a lack of caring for her staff and a lack of quality communication. Performance reviews were always late and negative, and staff meetings were seldom held. The data was summarized by the HRVP and reported to the president of the hospital and the president of the Board. The concerns were discussed and it was agreed that an important decision had to be made.

The options that were discussed were the following: 1. Should we put her on probation for the next ninety days to give her a chance to change her leadership style? 2. Should we offer her an early retirement package in an effort to remove her from her position? 3. Should we consider termination? I think it is important to point out that there was enough documentation to legally warrant termination. The documentation had been gathered during a period of months as a result of the meetings that where chaired by the HRVP. I think it is also important to point out that the nursing position in any hospital is a critical one and is associated with the hospital's mission statement for the purpose of giving the highest quality of care to its patients. When the nursing staff morale is low, quality patient care can be in jeopardy because the self-esteem of the nurses has been negatively affected. A person's self-esteem and motivation are closely tied together. There is a duality between these two behavioral definitions.

Upon discussing the findings with the VP of Nursing in a meeting between the HRVP and the president of the hospital and presenting the various options available to her, she decided to take the early retirement option.

The lesson to be learned from this is the following: This kind of behavioral leadership problem should not have been allowed to exist for as long as it did— several years. The problem should have been addressed by the VP of Nursing's supervisor and the president as soon as it became known that her leadership style within the Nursing Department was negative and autocratic. Her approach clearly had a direct negative affect upon their motivation, self-esteem, and overall daily performance.

A time line was established for her departure and the recruiting effort had begun to replace her with a qualified health care professional as quickly as possible. Once the nursing staff learned of her decision to retire, the morale quickly increased. Additionally, the rumors of a union campaign went away.

Once again, this case factually and clearly lends credence to the importance of modern leadership in health care and all organizations. There is no short cut to providing sound leadership principles and direction to teams. Leadership requires dedication, believability, and hard work by all managers who have the responsibility of leading teams of people.

Case Study B

HEALTH CARE ADMINISTRATOR/CEO

This specific case involves a large hospital and the Administrator/CEO who clearly did not understand the importance of providing complete, pro-active leadership for the hospital that he was responsible for, especially in the areas where there were obvious employee problems. He consistently displayed signs of burnout and avoidance behavior within the daily operation of the hospital. Employee problems were ignored and left to his direct reports to resolve in all departments in the hospital.

This health care institution was a non-union facility and in this regard the Human Resources vice president and his staff tried to maintain an open door policy for the employees in an effort to allow them to discuss their concerns or frustrations. This task, at times, became overwhelming in view of the fact that the administrator was not willing to address problems. Frustration and uncertainty had been building for several years.

Members of the Board of Directors had become aware of these significant problems and had begun to question why these issues weren't being addressed and resolved. The pressure had begun to build on the administrator and his overall behavior and leadership was being questioned. Numerous meetings were held with his direct reports in an effort to keep him up to date about employee concerns. During a period of time, he had begun to lose credibility among his direct reports and the employees of the hospital. His lack of leadership had become very obvious and very telling; employee morale was at an all-time low as a result of his behavior. He was spending much more time in his office and not focusing upon the serious problems that were being brought to his attention almost on a daily basis. Teamwork and quality communication among departments were clearly eroding and concerns were being expressed that these issues could affect the quality of care for patients. The administrator was more concerned with politics and pleasing the Board of Directors than he was with performing the important duties of his job as the administrator of the hospital.

Morale continued to decrease, turnover became a costly concern, employees were extremely frustrated that the very visible problems weren't being addressed and resolved. The morale of the majority of employees continued to decline. The hospital Board of Directors and the hospital administrator had begun to schedule several meetings to discuss various approaches to address and resolve these problems. After a number of monthly discussions with the Board of Directors, various effective options were discussed. It was agreed by the

Board of Directors and the hospital president to hire a management consultant in an effort to correct the problems within the hospital associated with the employee concerns.

Once the management consulting team was hired, they began with a fact-finding process in an effort to gather the accurate facts that had been referenced among the employees during the last eighteen months. For a period of three months, information was gathered to accurately focus upon the problems related to employee concerns and frustrations.

Once the data was formulated, assessed, and discussed it was agreed upon to schedule an Employee Attitude Survey. Another way to describe this important process is to call it an Employer Vulnerability Audit. This survey is an instrument that is used to ask employees to express their concerns with regard to the culture in which they work. It was agreed upon by the Board of Directors as well as the president of the hospital that schedules would be established and communicated to all employees that the process of completing the survey would be offered to them to express their opinions.

The process went forward and employees were made aware of the time they could choose to take the survey. This administrative process was met with a great deal of enthusiasm and receptivity. The general opinion within the hospital among the employees was that finally their concerns would be listened to and hopefully something would be done to improve the work environment. Once the schedule was communicated to all employees to include a date, location, and how to complete the attitude survey form, the employees began to arrive at the designated location to complete the form and place it in a sealed box. The form was designed to be confidential and therefore their names were not required on the form. This entire process required one week for all shifts to complete. Within the healthcare culture, the nursing department has three shifts to insure the patients are receiving the necessary care that they need. For planning purposes, the established schedule did allow for the second and third shifts to complete the survey form.

The overall purpose of conducting a confidential Employee Opinion Survey is threefold: 1) to find out the present level of employee morale for the organization and for each survey group, 2) to find out how effectively the organization is meeting the needs of employees toward job satisfaction, 3) to solicit employees' suggestions on what can be done to make the organization an even better place to work for everyone. The ultimate objective in conducting an Employee Opinion Survey is improvement in employee attitude and morale, improving the employer-employee relationship, and increasing overall efficiency in the quality of services provided.

The following topics are those the Employee Opinion Survey addresses in an effort to improve the work environment and improve the image of the organization:
- Top Management Attitudes toward Morale
- Supervisory Attitudes toward Employees
- Human Resource Policies
- Working Conditions
- Employee Benefits
- Compensation Polices
- Job Security

- Safety
- Complaint and Grievance Procedure
- Consistency of Organizational Rules and Discipline
- Leadership and Supervision
- Employee Handbook and Policy Manual
- Bulletin Boards

These are some of the key points and related questions used to determine how the employees really felt about working for their present employer. These same areas were referenced for the hospital employees when taking Survey.

Once the data was compiled and assessed it was very clear that hospital leadership needed to change their approach and the overall work environment if employee morale was to improve.

Various action plans were put into place by all management to make the necessary changes to accomplish these goals. The Board of Directors were made aware of the findings from the survey and had agreed to implement the various departmental action plans.

The key point of this case is to provide the necessary training and leadership necessary in order to meet the needs of all employees. There is no shortcut to accomplishing this goal. The leadership must start the top with the senior management members and communicate the objectives throughout the organization. This effort required believability, hard work, accountability, and purposeful communication, including an open door policy for all employees.

Case Study C

HOSPITALITY INDUSTRY

This case involves a large corporate hotel organization. Senior management in the hospitality industry is called the Executive Committee. The Executive Committee positions are the following: General Manager, Food and Beverage Director, Director of Engineering, Director of Housekeeping, Director of Human Resources, Director of Marketing and Sales, and Director of Finance. The size of the hotel/property is determined by the number of rooms that are available within each hotel. This specific case involved a large hotel consisting of close to a thousand rooms.

The problem that this case will be referencing is one associated with the Human Resources Department. This department was structured in such a way that each of the functions had a manager reporting to the Human Resources Vice President (HRVP). When the new HRVP was hired, he had to learn the various components of the culture and rebuild the team of Human Resources. Prior to doing this, of course, he had to get to know the various managers and the way they ran their individual departments and their style of managing and servicing the hotel. Once this was accomplished, he began to hold these managers accountable for meeting each of their goals on an annual basis. It is important to note that this hotel was non- union. In this kind of specific culture, it is important to meet the needs of each employee if possible and affordable.

The newly hired HRVP had begun to hold staff meetings once a week in which to discuss various action items that were assigned to each manager. This was a good way to communicate with each manager, to make the team stronger, and to provide important services to the hotel.

After a period of eight months, this approach had begun to be met with some resistance by several of the managers. It clearly became a political issue. This became evident when several of the managers made arrangements to have a private meeting with the general manager of the hotel. This meeting never involved the HRVP. This is not the professional way to resolve the situation. It is important to note that this approach to running the Human Resource Department was a mandate established by the general manager to the HRVP upon being hired.

In summary, what *should* have happened and *didn't* is the following: The general manager should have involved the HRVP in meetings with the hotel general manager to insure the concerns being expressed were accurate and not political or emotional. In business, there are always many sides to a story. Leadership in any business should involve purposeful communication in an effort to insure that people are treated fairly and professionally and with dignity. This did not happen in this case.

What should have happened is the following: The hotel general manager should have made an effort to retrieve all the facts related to the allegations that were being made by several of these managers toward the HRVP. He didn't do this. Also, a meeting should have been facilitated by the general manager, the HRVP, and the managers to find out the facts.

The key lessons here includes the importance of providing leadership, objectivity, purposeful communications, and time to find out the facts involving the allegations. The general manager's approach was wrong and ineffective. The outcome was a poor one in the sense that the truth was never determined and the managers were never held accountable.

The HRVP became frustrated and disappointed upon learning of the meetings that did not include him. After a period of two or more years, he had resigned for another position.

Case Study D

HEALTH CARE

his case addresses the need to insure that employee performance reviews are conducted on time, all the time. This particular hospital employed three hundred full-time people and one hundred part-time people. In this hospital, the senior management staff included the following professionals: The President, Vice President of Nursing, Vice President of Finance, Human Resources Vice President, Director of Engineering/ Maintenance, Director of Dietary, Director of Housekeeping, and the Director of the Medical Staff.

For a period of several years, the employee performance review system was not being administered on a timely basis. This was allowed to happen because the president did not provide the necessary leadership to insure the performance review process was being administered correctly and on time for all employees. He allowed the system to fail by not mandating to his direct reports that the process must be changed and given the priority it warrants. When this was allowed to happen, employee morale was clearly affected. When morale is affected, motivation is also affected and decreased. The employees begin to think that senior management doesn't care about their individual performance reviews. This thought process begins to become a normal discussion among employees and it has a far-reaching affect in the following areas:

- Morale is affected.
- Motivation is affected and decreased.
- It may affect turnover.

Very possibly there may be private discussions being held with regard to establishing a union; union cards may begin to be seen in the hospital.

In summary, the situation becomes very seriously problematic. This kind of problem can be avoided in all organizations, especially in this case, if senior management had given this important Human Resources system priority. Statements one through three above are just only a few problems that could emerge as a result of the performance review process not being given the priority it warrants. Some of the reasons why this does happen are the following:

Managers at all levels may not be trained to conduct a performance review interview.

Senior management has not communicated and emphasized the importance of performance reviews—that they be completed on a timely basis.

The administrative system may be flawed in the sense that the Human Resources Department doesn't send out the reviews to various departmental managers on a timely basis causing a backlog.

Departmental managers may not exercise good time management skills in which to give this important employee administrative process priority.

At this point, I think it is also important to reference the steps the manager should take to prepare for the performance review meeting with a subordinate:

- The reviewing manager should schedule the time with the employee at least one week in advance. The scheduled time should be communicated to the employee with regard to the date, time, and location.
- The reviewing manager should thoroughly prepare by studying the employee's file and any other related documentation to insure the review process is complete and professional.
- The reviewing manager in my view, should consider going through a mental rehearsal, reviewing all of the employee's information and preparing to greet the employee in a very friendly and professional manner.
- The manager should also consider not sitting behind a desk. This may make the employee feel uncomfortable and create an awkward, adversarial environment.
- The preparation process should include making the employee feel at ease and comfortable.

- Lastly, it is important to understand that this process embraces purposeful communication whereby there is a sender of information and a receiver of information. And then the roles of the manager and the subordinate are reversed for the purpose of establishing two-way communication.

The Employee Performance Review Process is one of the most important administrative functions a manager has within his or her role as a manager. With regard to the employee's perspective, the employee looks forward to this meeting to better understand his or her overall performance—what the employee did well and what needs to be improved upon. The discussion between these two individuals should involve as many details as possible regarding the performance review. The review, in many cases, would involve the twelve months since the last performance review was conducted. Many organizations review their employees on a rolling twelve-month basis. In preparation for the next twelve months or the next review period, departmental objectives should be put in writing to include the objectives, the date for completion, the resources needed to complete the objectives— equipment, budgeted money, additional people. Once agreed upon, both the manager and the employee should sign the review form to confirm agreement. If the overall performance review should warrant a financial increase for the employee, based upon the organization's internal compensation system for performance, then an increase should be given if warranted. The key point: Employee Performance Reviews should never be late.

Care Of The Patient Is The Highest Priority

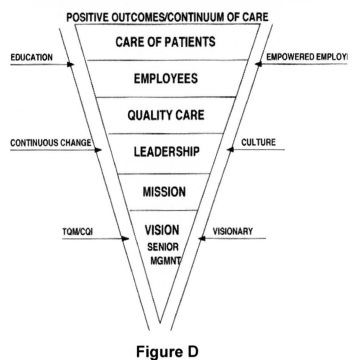

Figure D

Case Study E

HIGH TECHNOLOGY— BUSINESS EQUIPMENT

This case is unique and interesting because it involves a high technology manufacturing, sales and marketing organization. The manufacturing plant is non- union. In this regard, the management staff have worked very hard to insure that the plant remains non-union. During the recent years there have been attempts to unionize this particular plant but they were unsuccessful.

The senior management staff organizationally consists of the following: President, Vice President of Finance, Vice President of Marketing, Human Resources Vice President (HRVP), Vice President of Manufacturing, Vice President of Engineering, and a Vice President of Research and Development. The organization employs six hundred people at this location. The president reports directly to the president of the corporation located in another state.

Financially, this plant is doing very well and is very stable. They have avoided lay- offs for quite some time. Conversely, as an important point of reference for this case, the organization was still hiring people for certain hourly positions in manufacturing and administrative positions, and a number of professional positions. This is always a financial measurement of how the organization is doing economically.

One of the major concerns that the senior management consistently expressed was the continuous need to improve morale, especially among the hourly employees. Brainstorming sessions were held in order to find ways to accomplish this. The Human Resources Director (HRD) who was charged with doing this was constantly finding a logical and responsive way to keep morale high. In this regard, a quarterly Employee Communications Meeting was introduced and scheduled in an effort to improve communication and maintain a high degree of morale. This process of scheduling meetings continued for a three-year period and the results were excellent. The hourly employees would be selected by their department manager on a rotating basis and would attend prepared to ask questions regarding any topic they felt was important. The questions were generated from each employee in each of the departments and given to the person selected to attend the meetings.

The meeting would start by the HRD welcoming each of the employees to the meeting, which would be no longer than an hour. In attendance was a Human Resources secretary who would record in shorthand all the questions that were asked. When able, the HRD would answer questions as completely as possible. Once the meeting was finished, the questions would be reviewed during the following week and each of the questions would be answered thoroughly. Questions and answers would be typed utilizing a report format and posted on all bulletin boards as an effective way to communicate with all employees.

Due to the emergence of difficult economic business conditions for the company, a new performance review compensation policy was mandated for all six hundred employees. The HRD was given the difficult responsibility of communicating and administering this policy. It was a nightmare to say the least! The HRVP, also located at this facility, did not assist in any way. This situation became political and very problematic. All of the other senior management staff for each department and their direct reports would not accept the new policy easily. This being the case, the major responsibility for administering it was placed upon the HRD without any support. The hourly employees were very upset and would not accept this policy whatsoever! This affected morale, motivation, attitudes, and quality of the work. Hourly employees especially became extremely negative.

After several weeks, there was some loose talk of a union campaign within the hourly employees, mostly in the factory. This led to private union meetings at an alternate location. Some of the time these meetings would be held in restaurants or an employee's home. The situation escalated to the point that union authorization cards were seen in the plant requesting that employees sign them.

The corporate office, located several hundred miles away, became extremely concerned. After a short period of time, a law firm was hired in an effort to stop the union campaign. They were very professional and experienced. The attorneys scheduled numerous meetings with different groups of employees in an effort to determine the root cause of the effort to unionize.

The main reason was found to be the new compensation policy. The new policy was made in an effort to save money. A high percentage of employees would not get an increase for at least another year. This was very difficult if not impossible to accept. This disappointment led to other issues such as the health care policy, the internal promotion policy, the lack of effective leadership by the first line supervisors, not enough equipment and tools to do their job, and more. These became the emergent issues that were given to the attorneys.

Prior to all of this taking place, at the very beginning, the HRD strongly suggested that each of the senior management people hold group meetings to inform employees so they would better understand why the new policy had to be implemented. They were not receptive to this idea stating they were much to busy to be bothered with these kinds of meetings, that it was the Human Resources responsibility. Even the HRVP, once again, would not get involved.

This problem became serious and lasted for a period of a year. There were numerous meetings with all employees, coordinated by the HRD and the attorneys. This process became very time consuming and expensive. However, progress was being made in an effort to address the employees' concerns. The root cause of all the employees' discontent was related to the limited amount of money that had been budgeted for performance review and related compensation increases. This information was compiled and disseminated to all senior management as well as the corporate office.

Once analyzed, it was determined to reinstate the previous performance review schedule and to allocate whatever monies were necessary to have the union campaign stop. Additionally, many other issues were addressed: the health care plan, providing the necessary tools for the various departments, leadership training for the first line supervisors, and so on. When these changes were implemented, it eliminated all the selling points of the union campaign and the union eventually went away.

The lessons to be learned here are the following:

o Senior management should have been more responsible and should have scheduled all the necessary meetings in an effort to insure that employees understood the reasons for the change.
o The HRVP should have taken some of the lead to assist the HRD address these concerns.
o Plant-wide meetings should have been scheduled and held in an effort to address the many questions the employees had.

There is no substitute for pro-active leadership in an effort to meet the needs of employees. This can only be accomplished through commitment, effective communications, and a thorough understanding of the needs of the employees in each organization. This situation could have been avoided if leadership, professionalism, and common sense were utilized.

Case Study F

HIGH TECHNOLOGY-DEFENSE INDUSTRY

This case involves a high technology defense industry that organizationally was highly structured, reporting to the President of this division. Specifically, the direct reports were: Vice President of Manufacturing, Vice President of Engineering, Vice President of Human Resources, Director of Research and Development, Director of Public Relations, Vice President of Marketing, Vice President of Finance and a Director of Maintenance. The division was very successful technologically and financially. Their marketing programs were very effective and continually generated government contracted business. The plant facilities were modern and the necessary maintenance for equipment was always given priority to insure the equipment was operating safely and properly. All of the Occupational Safety Standards were strictly enforced and administered. The plant employed 1,500 people, of which 1,000 people were hourly employees and non-union.

The leadership style that was visible and well known by the president was mostly Theory X or "management by fear." This individual was very driven to be successful and did everything he could to utilize this management style when overseeing his direct reports. When senior management staff meetings were conducted, the president was clearly in control and was very demanding in the manner in which he conducted the staff meetings that lasted on the average of four to five hours.

The meetings were productive in the sense that a great deal of information was shared by each of the senior management staff. This was completed by giving a semi- formal presentation and giving copies to each of the management members in attendance for review and future reference. The senior management staff became concerned and somewhat frightened by this type of management style. However, they needed to work and many of them had been there many years so they tolerated this type of behavior by the president and did the best that they could under these circumstances. Although very difficult at times, they performed to the best of their ability.

In a period of time, the hourly employees became disgruntled, frustrated, and unhappy because of how they perceived they were being treated by the group leaders and first line supervisors. This unhappiness continued to grow and became very visible based upon the changing attitudes that were being displayed by the hourly employees. The plant had two shifts scheduled in order to meet production requirements for its defense contract customers.

The Human Resources Director and others within the Human Resources Department continually reported that the hourly employee unhappiness was continuing to grow. These reports were given to the president, the vice-president of Human Resources, and all other senior management members.

These reports were given over a period of time at the scheduled senior management staff meetings in detail.

The Human Resources Department strongly recommended that leadership training be scheduled for all management staff in addition to scheduling a formal Employee Attitude Survey for all employees. The Employee Attitude Survey is a process in which a number of questions are asked about the overall environment in which the employees are working each day in all departments throughout the plant.

Once the Attitude Survey process is complete, the information is tabulated and reports are then disseminated to senior management for review and assessment. Once this information is reviewed and discussed, plans are then made to address concerns and correct them to improve morale and increase the motivation of the work force.

Once the plans and actions are finalized, employee meetings are scheduled to communicate plans in response to the findings from the Employee Attitude Survey findings.

In this case, all these steps were accomplished. The various changes were implemented, and very importantly, remove all the issues from the ongoing union campaign. These actions proved to be very successful. The union campaign went away and the running of normal operations for the business continued. The key lesson associated with this case is to not let the various problems go unaddressed this long. Purposeful and pro-active leadership is critical to insure that the needs of employees are met where possible and affordable. If this is done on a continuous basis, the problems that have been referenced in this case will not reach this level of seriousness.

Case Study G

INTERNATIONAL HIGH TECHNOLOGY BUSINESS EQUIPMENT COMPANY

This is an organization that continued to grow on an international basis because of their diversified, quality product offerings. They continue to penetrate and capture the market as a result of very sound marketing strategies, properly placed employees, hard work, and their research and development of new products for their existing and new customers. Because of their rapid growth, which included various acquisitions over a period of years, some of the various operations managers clearly did not have necessary leadership skills. This resulted in very poor management practices in several parts of the operation. The focus of this case will highlight the various leadership skills that appeared to be lacking in several managers, why this may have occurred, and what should have been done to correct these problems.

This specific situation involves a manager of an important manufacturing assembly operation at a distant location from the corporate office. He reports directly to the president of a division that is also based at the corporate office. The division president reports the president of the corporation. The manager of this important satellite location was part of the new acquisition several years ago. Technologically, he would appear to have the many skills needed to oversee the various products that are being ordered and assembled for different customers. During the last eighteen months, this manager was not following the established policies associated with quality standards. Once these sub-par products arrived at the corporate office manufacturing location and were inspected for quality purposes, they were found to be inadequate for shipping to the customers. This individual in charge is not willing to conform to all the quality standards that have been established by the corporation. In this regard, products continued to be shipped that were not meeting quality standards. These issues continued to be addressed with this manager; however, he continued to perform in the same manner and was not willing to make any changes. The division president to whom he reported had made an effort to address these performance problems without taking any disciplinary action. This is clearly a serious operational mistake! The manager should have been warned that if he didn't improve his performance and meet the corporate quality standards, more progressive discipline would be administered and a complete set of chronological documentation would be placed in his file. Additionally, the division president is displaying avoidance behavior by not addressing the root causes of the performance problems.

This organization has a quality reputation to maintain that is known throughout the industry. There is a possibility that this manager does not have the leadership skills necessary to be responsible for the scope of this type of operation. If this is the case, he should either be put on probation, reassigned or terminated for cause. It is important to note, the detailed and complete documentation of such a case should always be done and placed in the employee's file.

These options would be reasonable ones to address this kind of attitude and behavioral performance problem. The documentation of these kinds of cases should always be placed in an employee's file for many reasons of potential litigation. We live in a society where these kinds of cases could go to court. Once again, if this individual's attitude and overall behavior with regard to performance and becoming a team player doesn't improve, some form of discipline should be administered.

The key lesson within this case is to not let this kind of performance issue go unaddressed once the problem is known.

Case Study H

A VERY WELL-KNOWN UNIVERSITY

This specific case references an academic culture of a large well-known university. The specifics of the case are related to several full-time faculty members and the various strategic planning meetings that were held by the Dean to discuss plans for the forthcoming school year. The Dean, of course, would always chair the meeting. The agenda for the meeting was prepared in advance and disseminated to all the full- time faculty members who were invited to attend the meeting so that they would be prepared to discuss the various relevant topics during the two-hour meeting.

As these cordial meetings began, each of the topics were addressed and each of the faculty members were encouraged to participate as fully as possible. Most of the topics were thoroughly discussed and appropriate actions items were assigned by the Dean to insure progress; closure would be made on a timely basis.

The faculty members were very qualified to teach the courses that were assigned to them and many had achieved tenure with this university; that in itself was an accomplishment. Acquiring tenure required a great deal of time for research of the chosen topic and the related writing to prepare for publishing, which was very time consuming. When this would occur, which it did for many, this would clearly take away time for preparation of their lectures in the classroom. It is my very strong view that this is not fair to the students.

In each classroom, there is nothing more important than ensuring students that their learning experience is as positive and complete as possible. The acquisition of purposeful and realistic knowledge should be the highest priority for all faculty members. Upon observing this on so many occasions, it became very concerning that the students were not getting the quality lectures they were expecting. This was supported by a certain percentage of students expressing concern quite often. This type of teaching behavior should never be allowed to exist. All students deserve and need an environment that gives them the opportunity to learn. Learning involves having a teacher who is totally committed to understanding their needs. The committed teacher establishes an environment in the classroom and during office hours whereby all students look forward to each of the scheduled lectures because they know they will learn something new.

Upon addressing the topic of office hours that each full-time faculty member was scheduled to hold, a certain percentage of the faculty treated this very lightly. This, too, was an opportunity to insure that each of the students can depend on these faculty members if needed.

The learning process is one of the most complex topics of the scholarly world. This case clearly supports the need for faculty members to become more committed to the students they are responsible to teach. All students deserve the very best that the each faculty member is able to give them. In many ways the teacher is a role model, mentor, and friend. Teachers provide the leadership in the classroom!

The Student Comes First

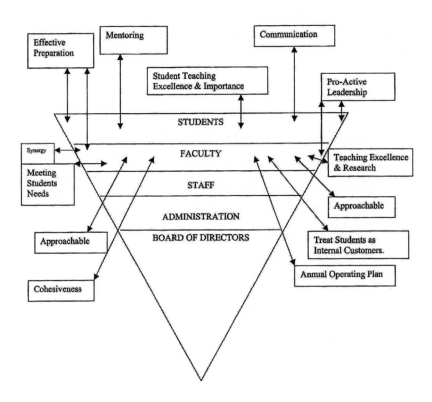

Figure H

Case Study I

New Hotel Opening

O nce the construction of a new hotel is completed, there are many plans that need to be implemented for a timely and successful opening.

Typically the plans begin at the corporate office and are then implemented by a team of experienced hotel professionals. The team of professionals hold the key positions for each of the disciplines that are typically referenced on an organization chart—human resources, food and beverage, housekeeping, rooms, marketing, finance, and engineering.

This specific case references a major hotel corporation that built a new hotel in a major city and had scheduled a specific date for the grand opening. Prior to this, as an important part of the planning process, was the purchase of furniture, bedding, kitchen equipment, food, and other items in preparation for a "soft opening." The purpose of the soft opening was to get the "bugs" out of the systems. Also an important part of the planning is the interviewing, hiring, orientation, and training of new employees.

In this particular case, there was a clear lack of leadership on the part of a corporate Human Resources person. This individual did not hold daily meetings with the key management members of the new hotel resulting in confusion, uncertainty, missed time-line dates. Motivation and morale declined, and the scheduled soft opening and grand opening dates were missed. Once these dates were missed, more money was needed to support the continuous cost of the opening.

The opening of a new hotel requires continuous communication, hard work, long hours, and sacrifices of all the employees involved to inspire its success.

This case clearly supports the important need for a strong, pro-active leadership if all the strategic goals are to be met. There's no place or room for politics and incompetence only leadership, if the organization is to be successful. Clearly, there was a significant need for more meetings to be held, daily if necessary, to make sure that all the important objectives were going to be met. Without purposeful communication, there is no leadership. This case clearly supports the need for quality communication by leaders.

Case Study J

CRUISE SHIP COMPANY

This case is associated with a very well-known cruise ship company and one of its key managers. The manager's scope of responsibility is for an important department aboard the ship called the spa and hair salon. This is a very active and popular department for all passengers when the ship is underway. This department always generates a significant amount of revenue every day for massages, hairstyling, manicures, and so on. Upon interviewing this manager, she clearly stated that "providing leadership on a cruise ship can be very intense; you play a mother figure also." Quite often, the staff who report to her become homesick. "So," she stated, "I have to come in and offer my support as their manager."

With regard to leadership, she stated, "We are on a never-ending journey of discovery; we must embrace new knowledge daily to motivate the staff and build strong teams."

During my interview with this manager, many topics were referenced to describe the culture on a cruise ship. The culture on a cruise ship is unique, therefore the leadership must be unique. Managers must be trained because they are from different countries. The training is scheduled and takes place very often to include topics like team building.

Because the morale of the staff is very important, meetings are conducted weekly to include passenger relations. These meetings include ice breakers that help the diversified crew members feel more comfortable during the meeting. The manager emphasized the importance of communicating with all her staff using the "open door policy" method to ensure they had access to her as often as they needed. Her first priority was a one-on-one approach and to be available at all times to help her people. She stated that building trust among her staff was critically important in order to have a strong team and to ensure that the department was running smoothly.

We discussed the importance of her role and her management style and her overall approach to her job. She stated that her job involved a lot of coaching and counseling to keep her staff motivated in addition to using daily praise. She felt that maintaining a positive attitude was an important characteristic in being a role model and a mentor. This type of leadership encouraged her staff to use the open door policy to freely express themselves. We ended our interview by her stating the following, "Then hitting a wall, we don't turn around and give up, we figure out how to climb it, or work around it."

This interview was insightful, informative, and realistic. It lended credence to what works effectively when building and motivating a team.

Case Study K

WHALE-WATCHING TOURIST BOAT INTERVIEW WITH THE SUPERVISOR

This specific case is associated with the crew of a whale-watching tourist boat in Alaska. The crew members of this whale-watching boat clearly stated the importance of leadership and working together. Through the ups and downs of certain jobs and work relations in their lives, they always turned back to the main characteristics in a boss/leader that have always boosted their morale, work ethic, and mood, and provided positivity as well as overall enjoyment of their daily work responsibilities.

The crew referenced the following areas that have a positive impact on their working environment.

- Encouragement
- Humility
- Patience
- Positive Attitude

- Hard Work
- Camaraderie

In their opinion, encouragement produces a craving to work hard. Humility creates an atmosphere whereby team work becomes second nature. The crew members went on to say that the lack of these characteristics creates a boss with an ego, hindering growth and work ethics.

Why patience? Patience is a special characteristic to have. A boss with patience prevents overwhelmed or stressed employees when performing their job. Patience can be a motivator to help employees to perform much better to improve morale.

Why a positive attitude? It's pretty obvious! The total vibe of the workplace changes, which causes the workers to enjoy working.

Why hard working? I have had a boss who wasn't hard-working at all. She didn't go the extra mile. She would always complain and only do what she had to do. This created an atmosphere of negativity and a feeling of unfairness.

The crew went on to comment, "Who would want to work harder if your boss was setting such a negative example?"

Camaraderie and teamwork? When a team is working well together it boosts everyone's morale!

"We work hard every day performing our duties as deck hands after the tourists leave the boat. We honestly don't think any of us could do it without having a 'team member' mind-set. Work is a blast if you're a team, no matter what you're doing."

The crew members went on to say what they look for in a boss. The boss should look for the good in people. The boss should respect them and encourage, them. "This is what our captain does very often. He has the best crew. We have confidence and love working hard for him. He treats his crew amazingly well and we respect him for this. When we make a mistake, we openly admit it without fear because he is very approachable and a genuine person. He thanks us daily for our efforts and that we are a crew on his boat. Now that is a great boss!"

This case clearly represents a realistic example of modern, pro-active leadership and what the measurable results can often be.

Additional Diagrams and Models

Employment Interview Steps Diagram

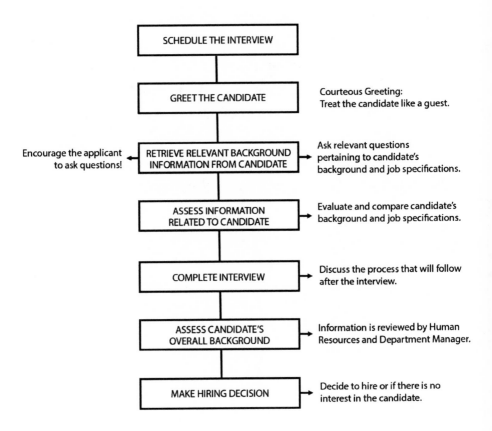

SCHEDULE THE INTERVIEW

GREET THE CANDIDATE

Courteous Greeting:
Treat the candidate like a guest.

Encourage the applicant
to ask questions! RETRIEVE RELEVANT BACKGROUND
INFORMATION FROM CANDIDATE

Ask relevant questions
pertaining to candidate's
background and job specifications.

ASSESS INFORMATION
RELATED TO CANDIDATE

Evaluate and compare candidate's
background and job specifications.

COMPLETE INTERVIEW

Discuss the process that will follow
after the interview.

ASSESS CANDIDATE'S
OVERALL BACKGROUND

Information is reviewed by Human
Resources and Department Manager.

MAKE HIRING DECISION

Decide to hire or if there is no
interest in the candidate.

Professional Interview Process Overview

Encourage the applicant to ask questions!

Ask relevant questions pertaining to candidate's background and job specifications.

Evaluate and compare candidate's background and job specifications.

Discuss the process that will follow after the interview.

Information is reviewed by Human Resources and Department Manager.

Decide to hire or if there is no interest in the candidate.

Professional Interview Process Model

The interview process should NOT be an interrogation! Each candidate should be treated as a guest of the organization.

Brainstorming Activity Sheet

Fill in the space after each statement.

I am "most talented" when I am:

_____

_____

I am "most likely to succeed" when I am:

_____

_____

I am "most versatile" when I am:

_____

_____

I am "best looking" when I am:

_____

_____

I am "class clown" when I am:

_____

_____

I am the "best dressed" when I am:

_____

_____

I am "best dancer" when I am:

_____

_____

I am "most friendly" when I am:

_____

_____

I am myself "best" when I am:

_____

_____

Worksheet accredited to Dr. Alex Osborn

Notes/Goals

Please use this page to record any ideas, thoughts, future goals, inspirations, etc. that come to your mind while reading through *On The Shoulders of Leaders*.

Author's Personal Note

"God is Watching Over Me"

With regard to my faith in God, I know that He is always watching over me. I know that He will carry me through many of my life's challenges and disappointments. There is always significant peace in knowing that He has a plan for my life as one of His children.

As the sun rises each day, God gives us a new beginning to enjoy and cherish all of His blessings. I will go forward with my life's journey to find peace within myself through Him and to enjoy every moment that He has blessed me with.

My faith will continue to be a promise of hope and a path between my heart and God.

I will always try to remember that I am one of God's children and His love for me will always be a part of my heart and He is never far away. God is Always Watching Over Me.

PROVERBS 3:13 - Wisdom Is Precious; Happy is the man that findeth wisdom, and the man that getteth understanding.

CPSIA information can be obtained
at www.ICGtesting.com
Printed in the USA
FFOW05n0118031116